Frommer's™

Dublin
day BY day™

1st Edition

by Emma Levine

John Wiley & Sons, Ltd

Contents

UK Publisher: Sally Smith
Executive Project Editor: Daniel Mersey (Frommer's UK)
Commissioning Editor: Mark Henshall (Frommer's UK)
Development Editor: Chris Bagshaw
Content Editor: Hannah Clement (Frommer's UK)
Cartographer: Tim Lohnes
Photo Research: Jill Emeny (Frommer's UK)

5   4   3   2   1

A Note from the Publisher

Organizing your time. That's what this guide is all about.

Other guides give you long lists of things to see and do and then expect you to fit the pieces together. The Day by Day guides are different. These guides tell you the best of everything, and then they show you how to see it *in the smartest, most time-efficient way*. Our authors have designed detailed itineraries organized by time, neighborhood, or special interest. And each tour comes with a bulleted map that takes you from stop to stop.

Hoping to tour the best in Georgian architecture, stroll down Grafton Street, or taste your way through gourmet Dublin? Planning a walk through Trinity College, or plotting a day of funfilled activities with the kids? Whatever your interest or schedule, the Day by Days give you the smartest routes to follow. Not only do we take you to the top attractions, hotels, and restaurants, but we also help you access those special moments that locals get to experience—those "finds" that turn tourists into travelers.

The Day by Days are also your top choice if you're looking for one complete guide for all your travel needs. The best hotels and restaurants for every budget, the greatest shopping values, the wildest nightlife—it's all here.

Why should you trust our judgment? Because our authors personally visit each place they write about. They're an independent lot who say what they think and would never include places they wouldn't recommend to their best friends. They're also open to suggestions from readers. If you'd like to contact them, please send your comments my way at mspring@wiley.com, and I'll pass them on.

Enjoy your Day by Day guide—the most helpful travel companion you can buy. And have the trip of a lifetime.

Warm regards,

Michael Spring, Publisher
Frommer's Travel Guides

About the Author

Bradford-born and with Dublin roots, **Emma Levine** spent eight years living, working, and travelling in Asia as an author and photographer, specialising in cricket culture in India and Pakistan. Attention then turned to strange sports in Kyrgyzstan and Iran, and another book and TV series later she returned to England, and is now based in London. With itchy feet rarely soothed, Emma writes travel guides (and thankfully still travels) to far-flung cities around the world, still loving adventures and following sport.

Acknowledgments

Special thanks to Sinead Barden at Dublin Tourism, my tolerant host Ethel, and wonderful Dublin tour guide Heather (my cousin).

An Additional Note

Please be advised that travel information is subject to change at any time—and this is especially true of prices. We therefore suggest that you write or call ahead for confirmation when making your travel plans. The authors, editors, and publisher cannot be held responsible for the experiences of readers while traveling. Your safety is important to us, however, so we encourage you to stay alert and be aware of your surroundings.

Star Ratings, Icons & Abbreviations

Every hotel, restaurant, and attraction listing in this guide has been ranked for quality, value, service, amenities, and special features using a **star-rating system.** Hotels, restaurants, attractions, shopping, and nightlife are rated on a scale of zero stars (recommended) to three stars (exceptional). In addition to the star-rating system, we also use a **kids** **icon** to point out the best bets for families. Within each tour, we recommend cafes, bars, or restaurants where you can take a break. Each of these stops appears in a shaded box marked with a coffee-cup-shaped bullet ☕ .

The following **abbreviations** are used for credit cards:

AE	American Express	DISC	Discover	V	Visa
DC	Diners Club	MC	MasterCard		

Frommers.com

Now that you have this guidebook to help you plan a great trip, visit our website at **www.frommers.com** for additional travel information on more than 3,500 destinations. We update features regularly to give you instant access to the most current trip-planning information available. At Frommers. com, you'll find scoops on the best airfares, lodging rates, and car rental bargains. You can even book your travel online through our reliable travel booking partners.

A Note on Prices

In the "Take a Break" and "Best Bets" sections of this book, we have used a system of dollar signs to show a range of costs for one night in a hotel (the price of a double-occupancy room) or the cost of an entrée (main meal) at a restaurant. Use the following table to decipher the dollar signs:

Cost	Hotels	Restaurants
$	under $100	under $10
$$	$100–$200	$10–$20
$$$	$200–$300	$20–$30
$$$$	$300–$400	$30–$40
$$$$$	over $400	over $40

An Invitation to the Reader

In researching this book, we discovered many wonderful places—hotels, restaurants, shops, and more. We're sure you'll find others. Please tell us about them, so we can share the information with your fellow travelers in upcoming editions. If you were disappointed with a recommendation, we'd love to know that, too. Please write to:

Frommer's Dublin Day by Day, 1st Edition
Wiley Publishing, Inc. • 111 River St. • Hoboken, NJ 07030-5774

12 Favorite
Moments

12 Favorite **Moments**

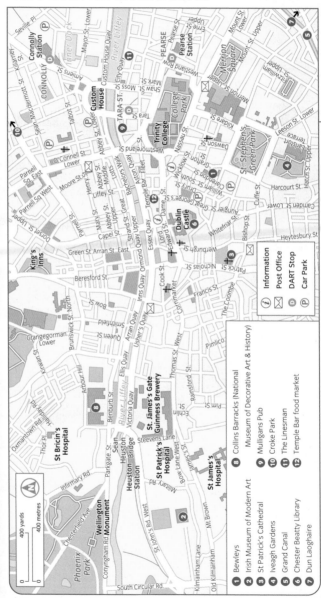

1. Bewleys
2. Irish Museum of Modern Art
3. St Patrick's Cathedral
4. Iveagh Gardens
5. Grand Canal
6. Chester Beatty Library
7. Dun Laoghaire
8. Collins Barracks (National Museum of Decorative Art & History)
9. Mulligans Pub
10. Croke Park
11. The Linesman
12. Temple Bar food market

Information

ⓘ Information
☒ Post Office
Ⓓ DART Stop
Ⓟ Car Park

400 yards
400 metres

I've seen Dublin go through a huge transformation over the last few decades to reveal its many facets: from 1970s gloomy unemployment to 1990s buoyant Celtic Tiger and its 21st-century modern incarnation. Today, Dublin is all about cutting-edge design, sky-high property prices, sophisticated wine-bars, and a multicultural workforce. But some things don't change: the Croke Park crowds, love of a drink, great sense of humor, respect for its historical heroes, cheerful cynicism of the government, and frustration with traffic jams. I'm hoping that these favorite moments will still be possible in another few decades.

① **Sipping coffee on Bewley's balcony.** The tiny 3rd-floor balcony overlooking Grafton Street is perfect to sip a coffee and watch the world swarm beneath. Thankfully it's now one of many places in Dublin to get a decent cup of strong coffee, but Bewley's was the first and will always be a favorite. *See p 102.*

② **Wandering through sculptures at the IMMA.** The 17th-century Royal Hospital Kilmainham, once housing retired soldiers, is now home to the Irish Museum of Modern Art. Wander round huge sculptures in the courtyard in what's a fine use for an old hospital. *See p 68.*

③ **Watching the sunlight inside St Patrick's Cathedral.** Late afternoon usually means organ practice for Evensong in the grand cathedral. As the sun starts dipping in the late afternoon, watch the colors on the walls as the light shines through the stained-glass windows. *See p 11.*

④ **Wooded walks and derelict statues at Iveagh Gardens.** So close to popular St Stephen's Green and yet a world away, this secluded Victorian garden has a cascade, statues with no arms, fountains, and shady woods—perfect for a peaceful afternoon. *See p 88.*

Bewley's busy exterior.

⑤ **Morning stroll along the Grand Canal.** This walk takes you close to the main road and yet this canalside path seems miles away from traffic. Take a stroll on a Sunday as the city is waking up, and if the sun is shining then the ducks will waddle out and bask in the sun. I love the locks, the willow trees, and the view of Peppercanister Church from Huband Bridge. *See p 62.*

⑥ **Musing the manuscripts at Chester Beatty Library.** One of my favorite exhibitions and venues. Instead of the mammoth queues for

The Croker Crowds.

the Book of Kells, step into the tranquillity of the *Sacred Traditions* display of illuminated manuscripts, ancient texts, and miniature paintings from around the world. *See p 14.*

❼ Smelling the sea at Dún Laoghaire. When I was a small child, we would drive along the coast to watch the boats in Dún Laoghaire. Now there's the speedy DART, the wonderful coastal suburban train that makes the journey even better. Step off the train and start smelling the sea. *See p 148.*

❽ Exploring the aisles at What's In Store. This is the best part of Collins Barracks. Now housing the National Museum of Decorative Arts and History, you can find thousands of exhibits crammed into tall display cases at the What's In Store section, from samurai swords to silver. On each visit I notice some different treasures. *See p 57.*

❾ Deciding where serves the best pint of Guinness. Need I say more? Guinness might be available the world over, but it really does taste better over here. Mulligans? Cobblestone? Ryans? Hard to tell, but it's always a good moment watching the pint being slowly pulled and then settling, ready to be sunk. *See p 115.*

❿ The crowd at the Croker. I've been to many sporting venues around the world, but Croke Park for hurling or Gaelic football is one of the greatest. The fun starts on seeing both sets of supporters, most clad in their team's shirts, walking together up O'Connell Street and stopping in every pub along the way. And the riot of color and noise when the teams emerge onto the pitch is spine-tingling stuff. *See p 132.*

⓫ Looking at the Linesman on the Liffey. I love life-sized sculptures, of which Dublin has many, from noble portraits of Daniel O'Connell in City Hall to a grinning Brendan Behan on the Royal Canal. The Linesman hauls the ropes from the Liffey in Sir John Rogerson Quay, probably thinking how much the surroundings have changed over the years. *See p 52.*

⓬ Enjoying the new "foodie" culture. It's so good to see Dublin starting to take its food seriously. Food markets are starting to spring up, so visit the one in Temple Bar to choose cheeses, sample ciders, and cast your discerning eyes over the cookies. At last there are more options (and decent ones) for eating out in Dublin. *See p 84.* ●

Choosing cheese at Temple Bar food market.

The Best **in One Day**

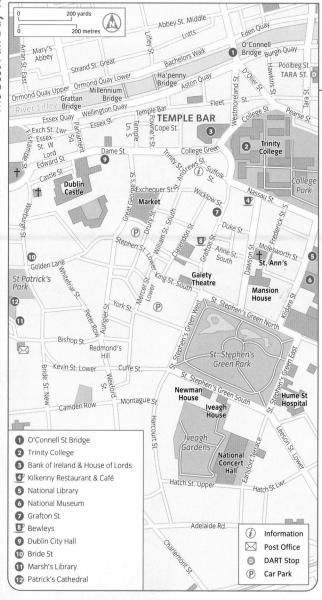

0 _____ 200 yards
0 _____ 200 metres

1 O'Connell St Bridge
2 Trinity College
3 Bank of Ireland & House of Lords
4 Kilkenny Restaurant & Café
5 National Library
6 National Museum
7 Grafton St
8 Bewleys
9 Dublin City Hall
10 Bride St
11 Marsh's Library
12 Patrick's Cathedral

i Information
✉ Post Office
D DART Stop
P Car Park

This full day kicks off with some of Dublin's most famous landmarks, including a few museums and galleries. You might not be in the mood to see them all, but the beauty of Dublin being so compact is that you'll probably find yourself retracing your steps on another day and so have time to visit any place you left out. Dublin is a walking city, with no real need for public transport. All you need are comfortable shoes—and waterproofs. START: **All cross-city buses to O'Connell St.**

1 ★ kids O'Connell Street Bridge. Stand on the north side of O'Connell Bridge by the statue of Daniel O'Connell, and you're in what many Dubliners believe is the very heart of the city. The man himself, cast impressively in bronze (see p 25), was a politician and patriot in the 1800s and the first Catholic to enter the House of Commons. Edge past the photo-taking groups and look for the bullet holes in the angels that ring the base of the statue. Look north to see the huge stainless steel Millennium Spire (commonly known as The Spike, *see p 18*) and cross the River Liffey over O'Connell Street Bridge. The bridge is unique in Europe: a multi-lane traffic highway, it is even wider than it is long. ⏱ *15 min. Bus: All cross-city buses.*

2 ★★ kids Trinity College. Ireland's oldest university, founded in 1592 by Queen Elizabeth I, is an oasis of lawns, cobbled paths, and architecture ranging from the 1700s to the 1900s. Flanked by the two statues of old boys Oliver Goldsmith (1728–1774) and Edmund Burke (1729–1797), walk through the main entrance to the white Campanile, a famous college sight. Explore the 16 hectares (40 acres) of grounds, and remember you're on the hallowed turf of the establishment that educated the likes of Oscar Wilde, Bram Stoker, and Samuel Beckett. There's probably a huge queue snaking around the huge Old Library to view the famous Book of Kells,

the illuminated manuscript dating back to AD 800. If you have the time, I recommend returning another day to see Trinity and the Book of Kells in more detail. (See *Special Interest Tours: Trinity College, p 36*) ⏱ *1 hr. College St.* ☎ *01-896 1000 (gen). www.tcd.ie. Mon–Fri 7am–midnight; Sat, Sun & hols 8am–6pm. Bus: All cross-city buses.*

3 ★★ Bank of Ireland and House of Lords. Opposite the Trinity entrance, the sweeping colonnade marks the entrance to the Bank of Ireland. It was originally constructed in 1729 as the House of Commons—the first purpose-built Parliament House in the world. Designed by Edward Pearce, later knighted, it was converted into the banking HQ following the 1800 Act of Union, which meant

Edmund Burke stands guard outside Trinity College.

Top Attractions: Practical Matters

Dublin Pass: This smartcard (www.dublinpass.ie) gives you free entry to over 30 top attractions, including Christ Church Cathedral, Dublin Castle, Dublin Zoo, Guinness Storehouse, GAA Museum, and St Patrick's Cathedral. For those attractions that have free admission anyway, the Pass usually offers a free info pack or discounts in the restaurant. Buy online (allow time for postage) or at Dublin Tourism's head office on Suffolk Street. If you buy at Dublin airport's tourist office, it includes a free bus journey to the city. The Dublin Pass is valid for 1 (€31), 2 (€49), 3 (€59), or 6 days (€89). Reduced price for kids.

that the country would be governed from London. The House of Lords still survives; visit its oak-paneled interior and check out the huge 18th-century chandelier with more than 1,000 pieces of crystal and tapestries depicting historical scenes. With few visitors, the curator usually has time to give you decent information. ⏱ *30 min. 2 College Green.* ☎ *01-677 6801 ext 3369. Free admission. Mon–Wed & Fri 10am–4pm; Thur 10am–5pm. 30-min guided tours Tues 10.30am, 11.30am & 1.45pm. Bus: All cross-city buses.*

The colonnaded Bank of Ireland.

4 ★ **kids Kilkenny Restaurant & Café.** Located on the 2nd floor of Kilkenny (see p 82) (you'll be tempted to return for a gift-buying spree), this is great for coffee, cakes, sandwiches, hot meals, or even a full Irish breakfast before 11am. It also has gluten-free dishes, which seem the norm now in Dublin. *5/6 Nassau St.* ☎ *01-677 7075. $.*

5 ★★ **National Library.** Opened in 1890, this holds more than 1,000 manuscripts and nearly 100,000 books, including rare first editions of Joyce and Yeats. For visitors with no intention of reading, go for the magnificent stained-glass windows in the entrance depicting luminaries in the worlds of literature and philosophy, the wooden carvings on the staircase, and the vast domed reading room. Today's readers might be using laptops, but it's easy to imagine the same scene from a century ago. The Genealogy Service is a great resource for tracing Irish roots, where any visitor can get initial help from expert staff. The library also has exhibition rooms and a good café, with occasional lunchtime literary events. ⏱ *30 min. Kildare St.* ☎ *01-603 0200. www.nli.ie. Free admission. Mon–Wed 9.30am–9pm; Thurs & Fri*

9.30am–5pm; Sat 9.30am–1pm. Bus: Inc 7, 8, 10 & 11.

6 ★★★ **kids** **National Museum.** One of three National Museums in the city, all of them free, this one is devoted to archaeology. At the main entrance, don't miss the wonderful mosaic floor depicting the 12 signs of the zodiac. Once inside, highlights include Iron Age bog bodies discovered in 2003. Amazingly preserved, you can still see the leather-plaited armband with a Celtic ornament on one of the bodies. The Treasury has exhibits from the early Middle Ages, which was the Golden Age of Irish Art, including the renowned Ardagh Chalice and Tara Brooch. Kids can pick up activity sheets from the ticket office. When you've finished wandering around the comfortably small museum, stand and look out over the balcony at the intricate wrought-iron of the entire hall. ⏱ *90 min. Kildare St.* ☎ *01-677 7444. www.museum.ie/archaeology. Free admission. Tues–Sat 10am–5pm; Sun 2pm–5pm. Guided tours €2 (under 16 free). Tues–Sat 3.30pm & Sun 2.30pm. Bus: 7, 8, 10 & 11.*

7 ★★★ **kids** **Grafton Street.** It's time to take a walk down Dublin's pedestrianized, famous and fashionable street—usually the most crowded. Once it was Irish

Door knocker to the National Museum.

stores dominating consumers' choice; these days it's well-known British chain stores. At its southern end, at the entrance to St Stephen's Green, is the grand Royal Fusilier's Arch. Mid-way down, stop at Bewley's, famous for coffee since 1840, and little changed over the decades. Grafton Street is also the unofficial venue for hundreds of buskers; stroll up and listen to the musicians—the best ones usually playing in the early evening or at night. At any given time, there might also be a scattering of human "statues",

Quiet please: National Library reading room.

costumed, spray-painted, and standing very still on a box—something which quite remarkably gets people giving money. Try to see the (mainly) Georgian frontages behind the crowds, as most of these stores were originally built as private residences. At the southern end, you will be greeted by the statue of the Tart with the Cart, Dolly with the Trolley, or Trollop with the Scallops. Get the idea? Poor Molly Malone's ample cleavage did everything to encourage unkind nicknames. 🕐 *From 30 min. All buses to St Stephen's Green.*

🍵 ★ **Bewley's.** Still a Dublin institution, Bewley's Oriental Café has a choice of places to eat and drink. My favorite (probably in the whole of Dublin) is the 1st -floor café at a window seat overlooking Grafton Street, perfect for solitude, a newspaper, and an Americano. *78/79 Grafton St.* ☎ *01-672 7720. www. bewleyscafe.com $.*

⑨ ★★ **Dublin City Hall.** The huge rotunda of the City Hall, recently restored, is breathtaking. It was built in 1769 as headquarters for the city's

merchants, close to the trading hub Dame St (probably the very street you walked down) and is now used as council chambers. Its domed roof has gold-leaf embellishment, surrounded by four huge statues including Daniel O'Connell, and a marble mosaic of Dublin's coat of arms with the daunting motto "Happy the city where citizens obey". Down in the restored vaults is the interesting **Story of the Capital** multimedia exhibition. Divided into three sections, it covers Dublin's history from Viking times, through Georgian, and up to the present day. 🕐 *1 hr. Dame St.* ☎ *01-222 2204. Free admission to Rotunda. Exhibition: €4 adults, €2 students, €1.5 children. Bus: 77, 56A & 123.*

⑩ ★ **Bride Street.** If you're walking from City Hall to Marsh's Library, cut down Bride Street and pass Bull Alley on your right. This, like much of the area, was home to red-brick Victorian housing for the city's poor (now Liberties College), financed by philanthropist Lord Iveagh (Cecil Guinness). Across the road on Golden Lane, look up at the apartments, where scenes from Jonathan Swift's *Gulliver's Travels* are carved in relief on the upper levels. 🕐 *15 min. Bus: 50, 54A & 56A.*

Impressive statues circle City Hall's rotunda.

Leather-bound journals in Marsh's Library.

⓫ ★★★ **Marsh's Library.** A bibliophiles dream. Founded in 1701 by the splendidly named Archbishop Narcissus Marsh, this was Ireland's first public library and amazingly is still used for the purpose. Thankfully the place is usually pretty empty, save for a couple of helpful staff, so you can gaze down the aisle and marvel at the leather-bound tomes filling floor-to-ceiling dark oak bookcases. Look out for Jonathan Swift's death mask and the desk he probably sat at to write *Gulliver's Travels*. At the end, you can see the wired alcoves, or cages, where scholars were locked in with their rare books, preventing pilfering. Not that the library is a complete museum-piece—all the collection's 25,000 books, published between the 16th and 18th centuries, are now catalogued and available on the Internet. Visitors and researchers are welcome to request any book in advance and staff, perhaps wearing protective gloves if the book is valuable, will have it ready for your visit. ⏱ *45 min. St Patrick's Close.* ☎ *01-454 3511. www.marshlibrary.ie. Admission: €2.50 adults, €1.25 students & seniors, children free. Mon & Wed–Fri 10am–1pm, 2–5pm; Sat 10.30am–1pm. Bus: 50, 54A & 56A.*

⓬ ★★ 🅺🅸🅳🆂 **St Patrick's Cathedral.** Late afternoon is usually the best time to visit Ireland's largest church: the organ and choir often have a hearty practice before Evensong at 5.45pm and even the irreligious would find it spiritually uplifting, especially when shafts of light shine through the stained-glass windows. St Patrick (who was from Britain) baptized converts from paganism to Christianity close to here, and a small wooden church was built in his honor. The current cathedral dates from the 13th century and has been rebuilt many times since. Writer Jonathan Swift was its most famous dean, from 1713 to 1745. Look out for his grave and epitaph near the main entrance, standing up and facing the altar: this was relocated from a spot in the cathedral prone to flooding from the Poddle river. Still famous for its loud-pealing bells, the cathedral's choir took part in the first performance of Handel's *Messiah* in 1742. If the daily (Anglican) services don't appeal, try the organ recitals on most Wednesday evenings. ⏱ *1 hr. St Patrick's Close.* ☎ *01-475 4817. www.stpatrickscathedral.ie. Admission: €5 adults, €4 students, seniors, children. Free admission to services. Mon–Fri 9am–5pm; Sat & Sun: (Mar–Oct) 9am–5.30pm, (Nov–Feb) 9am–5pm. No admission during Sun services; 10.45am–12.30pm & 2.45–4.30pm. Call 01-453 9472 for other service times. Bus: 50, 54A & 56A.*

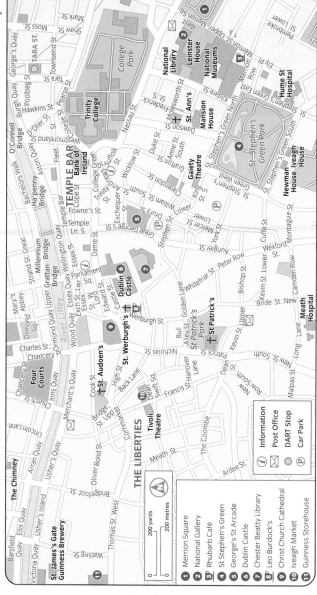

Moss St.
Mark St.
Shaw St.
George's Quay
Townsend St.
Poolbeg St.
Burgh Quay
Hawkins St.
Tara St.
Pearse St.
College St.
Westmoreland St.
Nassau St.
Frederick St. S.
Molesworth St.
Upper Merrion Sq.
West Merrion St.
Pembroke St. Lower
Leinster House
National Library
National Museums
Kildare St.
Merrion Row
Ely Pl.
Hume St. Hospital
St. Ann's
Mansion House
Dawson St.
Anne St. South
Duke St.
Grafton St.
St. Stephen's Green North
St. Stephen's Green
St. Stephen's Green East
Gaiety Theatre
King St. S.
St. Stephen's Green West
St. Stephen's Green South
Newman House
Iveagh House
O'Connell Bridge
Bachelors Walk
Ha'penny Bridge
Aston Quay
Fleet St.
College Green
TEMPLE BAR
Bank of Ireland
Suffolk St.
Wicklow St.
Cope St.
Fownes St.
Temple Ln. S.
Dame St.
Wicklow St.
Exchequer St.
Clarendon St.
William St. South
Mercer St. Lower
York St.
Aungier St.
Wexford St.
Cuffe St.
Montague St.
Great George's St. S.
Stephen St. Lower
Drury St.
Strand St. Great
Millennium Bridge
Grattan Bridge
Upper Ormond Quay
Essex Quay
Wellington Quay
Parliament St.
Essex St. W.
Lord Edward St.
Castle St.
Werburgh St.
Dublin Castle
St. Werburgh's
Whitefriar St.
Peter Row
Bishop St.
Bride St. New
Kevin St. Lower
Camden Row
Bull Alley St.
Golden Lane
St. Patrick's Park
St. Patrick's
Patrick St.
Kevin St. Upper
Dean St.
Mary's Abbey
Ormond Quay
Charles St.
Chancery Pl.
Four Courts
Inns Quay
Wood Quay
Merchant's Quay
Cook St.
High St.
St. Audoen's
Nicholas St.
Back Lane
Hanover Lane
Lamb Alley
Dean Swift Sq.
Francis St.
New Row South
New St. South
Long Lane
Malpas St.
Meath Hospital
Church St.
Lincoln Lane
The Chimney
Arran Quay
Ellis Quay
Usher's Quay
Usher's Island
Victoria Quay
Barsfield Quay
St. James's Gate Guinness Brewery
Watling St.
Thomas St. West
Oliver Bond St.
Bridgefoot St.
Bridge St. Upper
Cornmarket
THE LIBERTIES
Tivoli Theatre
Leo Burdock's
Meath St.
The Coombe
Ardee St.

River Liffey
College Park
Trinity College

200 yards
200 metres

Information ⓘ
Post Office ☒
DART Stop Ⓓ
Car Park Ⓟ

① Merrion Square
② National Gallery
③ Rhubarb Café
④ St Stephen's Green
⑤ George's St Arcade
⑥ Dublin Castle
⑦ Chester Beatty Library
⑧ Leo Burdock's
⑨ Christ Church Cathedral
⑩ Iveagh Market
⑪ Guinness Storehouse

After a full first day, the pace doesn't slow, although you can choose whether it's an in-depth look or a quick visit to many of these attractions. This tour stays in a similar area to the previous one, starting with a taste of Georgian Dublin in Merrion Square. This will be another day bringing you the best of art, history, and churches—finishing up with a pint of Guinness with a rather special view.

1 ★★ kids Merrion Square.

One of Dublin's most elegant Georgian squares, this was considered—and still is—the very best part of the city. Wander through the neat lawns and trees of its interior, Archbishop Ryan Park (see p 33) look out for the sculpture of Oscar Wilde reclining and gazing wistfully towards his childhood home, 1 Merrion Square (now the American University). Three sides of the square are lined with well-preserved Georgian houses, including *Number Twenty Nine* house museum (see p 30). The railings of the square are the venue of the wonderful weekend Art Market. ⏱ *45 min. Bus: 7, 10 & 45.*

2 ★★★ kids National Gallery.

I often find that long lines and crowds can dull the pleasure of visiting a great gallery. Not so here. This one is spacious, easy to get around, and relatively quiet—surprising considering some of the fantastic European paintings. There's a fine life-size sculpture of George Bernard Shaw from 1927, leading the way to the National Portrait Gallery. The Italian School includes masterpieces by Fra Angelico, Caravaggio, and Rubens. Huge works by Vermeer, Caravaggio, and Goya are my personal favorites, especially Caravaggio's *Taking of Christ*. Picasso, Monet, and Signac make up the French 20th-century school. Free activity packs are available for kids of all ages. ⏱ *90 min. Merrion Square West.* ☎ *01-661 5133. Free admission. Mon–Sat 9.30am–5.30pm; Thur 9.30am–8.30pm; Sun 12–5.30pm. Bus: 5, 10, 44.*

3 kids Rhubarb Café.

This little eatery represents Dublin's new brand of friendly cafés with coffee, paninis, and cakes. Small and cozy with a couple of outdoor tables, it gets busy at lunchtimes with local office workers. *18a Upper Merrion St.* ☎ *01-631 4924. www.rhubarb.ie. $.*

4 ★★★ kids St Stephen's Green.

This city center park was once the private gardens for local residents, each requiring a key to enter. It was landscaped by the head of Guinness in 1880 and since then has been a great public space with a huge pond where children feed the ducks (see p 88), a bandstand with music performed in summer, a small amphitheater, and sculptures and statues of prominent Dubliners. On sunny days, expect to see suited office-goers and students sprawled happily on the grass (which, strictly speaking, is not allowed). ⏱ *1 hr. See Best of the Outdoors p 87.*

The calm pond at St Stephen's Green.

⑤ ★ kids George's Street Arcade.

Dublin's first (and only) purpose-built Victorian shopping arcade, trade has fluctuated here since its opening in 1881. Once a meat market (the Market Bar was a sausage factory), these days its single aisle houses a quirky array of second-hand books, funky clothes, locally designed jewelry, deli-type foodstuff, cafés, and memorabilia. Gaze at its beautiful wrought-iron roof (gently restored to keep the original style), and the ornate red-brick Victorian façade, which comes out onto South Great George's St. ⏲ 30 min. Entrances on Drury St & South Great George's St. www.georgesstreetarcade.ie. Mon–Sat 9am–6.30pm; Thurs 9am–8pm; Sun 10am–6pm (not all stalls open on Sun). Bus: 77, 56A & 123.

⑥ ★ kids Dublin Castle.

Located in one of the oldest parts of Dublin, the castle's turbulent past encompasses Viking history, British Rule, fires, and rebellions, most of it having been rebuilt. Enter via the main gateway to the Great Court-yard, remains from the original castle built by King John of England in 1204, and gaze up at the Record Tower, the last intact medieval tower in Dublin. Visits are by guided tour only to the opulent rooms, including the State Rooms with the throne used for royal visits and the huge mahogany table used for diplomatic get-togethers. This table witnessed talks on the Good Friday (Belfast) Agreement, the 1998 groundbreaking treaty that finally brought peace to Northern Ireland. For me the most impressive part of the castle is St Patrick's Hall, the ceremonial centerpiece with ceiling paintings and family crests, used for inaugurating Irish presidents. ⏲ 1 hr. Dame St. ☎ 01-645 8813. www.dublincastle.ie. Admission: €4.50 adults, €3.50 concs, €2 children aged 6–12, under 6 free. Tours: May–Sept every 15 min; Oct–April every 30 min. Bus: 77, 49 & 123.

⑦ ★★★ Chester Beatty Library.

Stroll through the garden at the back of Dublin castle to this wonderful gallery. Bequeathed by art collector Sir Arthur Chester Beatty, it exhibits treasures from world cultures and religions. I especially love the peaceful ambience of the Sacred Traditions Gallery with illuminated centuries-old copies of the Koran, ancient Egyptian

Opulence of Dublin Castle.

love poems on papyrus, and intricately carved Japanese boxes. The Artistic Traditions gallery tells of the achievements of Beatty himself. Linger over a coffee at the 1st floor Silk Road Café (see p 109). ⏲ *90 min. Dublin Castle.* ☎ *01-407 0750. www. cbl.ie. Free admission. Mon–Fri 10am–5pm, Sat 11am–5pm, Sun 1– 5pm; Oct–Apr closed Mon. Bus: 77, 49 & 123.*

8 **kids** **Leo Burdock's.** Dublin's most famous fish and chip takeaway has been satisfying taste buds since 1913, making it the oldest "chipper" in town. The smoked cod is wonderful, especially with mushy peas. Basic flour-and-water batter is used. *2 Werburgh St.* ☎ *01-454 0306. $.*

9 ★ **kids** **Christ Church Cathedral.** One of Dublin's oldest landmarks, the cathedral dates back to 1030 although the present structure was built in the 1870s. Its aisles have seen many a congregant here, from Norman warrior Strongbow—who rebuilt it in stone and you can see a monument to him—to William of Orange, who donated treasures after his Battle of the Boyne victory in 1690. The cathedral choir took part in the world's first performance of Handel's Messiah in 1742, with the choir from neighboring St Patrick's. Its bells are the world's largest full-circle peal—listen out for their practice on Fridays 7–9pm. ⏲ *1 hr. Christchurch Place.* ☎ *01-677 8099. www.ccccdub. ie. Admission: €6 adults, €4 concs, children free. Jun–Aug 9am–6pm; Sep–May 9.45am–5 or 6pm. Bus: 49, 50, 51B & 77.*

10 ★ **kids** **Iveagh Market.** Walk down Nicholas St to look at the old Iveagh Market, built by Lord Iveagh in 1906. Now in disrepair, it appears that it will be refurbished and reopened—I certainly hope so. Look

Sleeping Bishop Lindsay in Christ Church Cathedral.

for the impish portrait on the corner, giving a cheeky wink. It's thought that this was none other than Lord Iveagh himself. *Between Francis St, Dean Swift Sq & Lamb Alley.*

11 ★ **kids** **Guinness Storehouse.** Firmly on the tourist trail, this former fermentation plant is in the heart of St James Gate Brewery— churning out Guinness since 1759. Huge, crowded, and lots of fun, the seven floors tell of the history, production, and advertising of the black stuff. Look out for the tasting lab explaining how different parts of the tongue taste its various elements. The 3rd floor has the excellent advertising campaigns from the 1980s, although I prefer the top floor old ads by John Gilroy. Your ticket gets you a free pint of Guinness at the Gravity Bar at the very top, with great 360˚ views of the city. Book online for a 10% discount and skip the queue. ⏲ *2 hr (including drink!). St James' Gate.* ☎ *01-408 4800. www.guinness-storehouse.com. Admission: €14 adults, students over 18 & seniors €9.50, students under 18 €7.50, children aged 6–12 €5, free for children under 7; family ticket €30. May–Sept 9.30am–7pm (last admission); Oct– Apr 9.30am–5pm (last admission). Bus: 51B, 78A & 123.*

The Best **in Three Days**

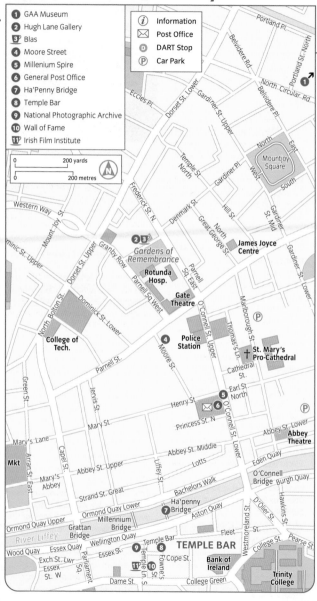

1. GAA Museum
2. Hugh Lane Gallery
3. Blas
4. Moore Street
5. Millenium Spire
6. General Post Office
7. Ha'Penny Bridge
8. Temple Bar
9. National Photographic Archive
10. Wall of Fame
11. Irish Film Institute

- (i) Information
- ⊠ Post Office
- Ⓓ DART Stop
- Ⓟ Car Park

This tour takes you north of the River Liffey, starting in the wonderful Croke Park for a sporting experience, and then has a long walk to the famous O'Connell St, ending up at Temple Bar. You'll be walking through busy shopping areas and so it's up to you how much time you want to spend.

① ★★★ **kids** **GAA Museum.** As a huge sports fan, this is one of my favorites. Part of the famous Croke Park Stadium and headquarters of the Gaelic Athletic Association, this tells the story of Gaelic games especially hurling and Gaelic football. The 15-minute video at the start of the tour shows the furious pace of hurling in action, which makes you realize what soft sports soccer or rugby really are. If you get to see a hurling match, it's easy to understand why it's been a theme in Irish heroic literature since the 18th century. The museum has jerseys, photos, and trophies dating back to 1871, and activities where you can use the hurley (like a hockey stick) to try and hit the ball—more difficult than it looks. An absolute must is the stadium tour, where you walk through the dressing rooms, VIP section, and corporate levels, with the guide giving its colorful history. The best moment of all is when you walk through the players' tunnel and onto the pitch. ⏰ *2 hr (including stadium tour). Croke Park, access via St Joseph's Ave.* ☎ *01-819 2323. www.gaa.ie/museum. Admission: €5.50 adults, student & seniors €4, children under 12 €3.50; €15 family ticket. Museum & stadium tour: €9.50 adults, student & seniors €7, children under 12 €6; €24 family ticket. Mon–Sat 9.30am–5pm, Sun & p/hols 12–5pm. Jul & Aug: Mon–Sat 9.30am–6pm. Tours: Every hour Mon–Sat 10am–3pm, Sun 1pm–3pm. Jul & Aug last tour 4pm. Bus: 3, 11, 16 & 46A.*

Stadium tour of Croke Park.

② ★★ **Hugh Lane Gallery.** It's quite a walk from Croke Park, so this spacious, relaxing gallery is a good place to wind down. Also known as the Dublin City Gallery, this has many Irish artists on display in a collection exceeding 2,000. Impressionist masterpieces include Manet's *Le Concert aux Tuileries*, Monet's *Waterloo Bridge,* and Renoir's *Les Parapluies* but check out Irish painters, especially Sean Scully's abstract creations and Jack B Yeats' oils. Highlight is the **Francis Bacon collection,** including the recreation of his London studio complete with paint-encrusted walls, piles of cans, and canvases everywhere. If you ever thought that you had an untidy house, go and look at his studio. Messy doesn't even start to describe it. It's great to know that such genius can indeed emerge from chaos. The gallery also hosts Sunday lectures and free concerts. (see *Arts & Entertainment p 127*) 🕐 *1 hr. Charlemont House, Parnell Square North.* ☎ *01-222 5550. www. hughlane.ie. Free admission. Tue–Thur 10am–6pm, Fri & Sat 10am–5pm, Sun 11am–5pm. Guided tours: Tues 11am & Sun 1.30pm. Audiotours: €3. Bus: 3, 10 & 13.*

3 **kids** **Blas.** On the gallery's 1st floor, this is one of the loveliest museum cafés around, with hot and cold dishes including steak, mushroom and Guinness pie. It also has a lovely little garden courtyard. *Hugh Lane Gallery, Parnell Square North.* ☎ *01-222 5550. $.*

4 ★ **Moore Street.** Once the city's most famous street market, Moore Street has diminished in size and quality over time but is still worth a look for an earthier Dublin shopping experience. (My late grandmother loved a bargain and came here for fruit and veg.) You can still see a few women selling bric-a-brac and the odd box of apples from old-fashioned prams. Its vendors now reflect Dublin's changing population, with more Asian and African stallholders selling foodstuff from sunnier climes. Look out for the horse-and-carts during morning delivery and listen out for the local banter. 🕐 *30 min. Moore St. Mon–Sat 8am–4pm. Bus: All buses to O'Connell St.*

5 ★★ **The Millennium Spire.** Replacing Nelson's Column, blown up in 1966 by the IRA, the Spire was the result of a long drawn-out planning process; so drawn out that it was three years late in welcoming the Millennium. Nonetheless, although most Dubliners think it's a total waste of money (€5 million), the 120m (395 ft) high stainless steel

The Millennium Spire has several nicknames including 'Stiletto in the Ghetto' and 'Poker near Croker'.

spire, 3m (10 ft) wide at the base and tapering to 15cm (6 inches) at the top, is the tallest city center structure and certainly hard to miss. Its appearance changes throughout the day; metallic blue at sunrise and sunset, shiny gray in the day, and black at night with tiny lights on the upper sections. As you'll have noticed, Dubliners love their nicknames: the more repeatable ones include the Spire in the Mire, Stiletto in the Ghetto, and Poker near Croker. *Bus: All buses to O'Connell St.*

6 ★★ **General Post Office.** The GPO (see **Dublin's Heroes** p 22) sits prominently on O'Connell Street, not only as a national institution but also central to the political and military turmoil of the 1916 Rising. Designed by Francis Johnston and built in 1814, its distinctive Doric columns span the five central bays, with John Smyth's statues of Fidelity, Hibernia, and Mercury above the portico. While buying your stamps inside the huge hall, take a look at the beautifully elaborate ceiling with Grecian designs. *An Post, O'Connell St. Counters open Mon–Sat 8am–8pm.*

⑦ ★ kids **Ha'penny Bridge.** The first pedestrian bridge over the River Liffey (and the only one until 2000) this iron bridge was built in 1816 and is one of Dublin's landmarks. Officially called the Liffey Bridge, and before that Wellington Bridge, its nickname came from the half-penny tax charged for each pedestrian to cross, which continued until 1919. Three lamps are supported by the curved ironwork over the walkway, recently renovated and repainted. Local folklore suggests that the tax was to keep the northern "riff-raff" away from the Southside. (There still remains some rivalry between those born in the north and south, the latter seeing themselves as far superior.) The loveliest time is in the late afternoon sun, with the long shadows of people walking over cast onto the side rails, or illuminated at night. *Bus: All buses to O'Connell St. Luas: Abbey St.*

Illuminated Ha'penny Bridge.

Sculptural detail on the GPO.

⑧ ★★ kids **Temple Bar.** Over the bridge brings you to Temple Bar, the street giving its name to a regenerated area and home to arts and entertainment since the early 1990s. Previously a forgotten edge of dockland, cheap rents brought an

Explore the bars, theatres and music venues in Temple Bar.

influx of the bohemian type, and so now there are bars, theaters, live music venues, and galleries aplenty. It's also the location of several new weekend markets. Most streets are narrow, cobbled, and with little traffic so it's a delightful area to wander around. Friday to Sunday is packed out with Hen and Stag parties (mainly from England), changing the ambience to a drinking fest (fancy-dress optional), with buskers and street performers. *www.temple-bar.ie*

⑨ ★★ National Photographic Archive. Part of the National Library's collection, this small gallery is the new home to more than 600,000 photographs, predominantly Irish. Its walls also host regularly changing exhibitions from the collection. Most of the negatives and transparencies have come from postcard and portrait studios throughout 20th-century Ireland. One of the most interesting is from the Keogh Collection in Dublin, 1915–1930, with photographs covering the political events and figures from those turbulent years. Visitors are allowed to access the archive. There is a small book and postcard store on the 1st floor. ⏱ *40 min. Meeting House Square, Temple Bar.*

☎ *01-603 0374. www.nle.ie. Free admission. Mon–Fri 10am–5pm, Sat 10am–2pm. Bus: All buses to Dame St or Wellington Quay.*

⑩ ★ kids Wall of Fame. Located appropriately opposite the Temple Bar Music Academy, this wall of huge photos captures the great and the good in Irish music. Taken mainly during the 1970s and 1980s by Irish photographers, the artists range from Shane McGowan (suitably clutching a bottle of booze) of the Pogues, Van Morrison, the late Phil Lynott, an unangelic-looking Bob Geldof, and of course U2, Ireland's most successful export. Stand on the street in the evening when the photos are lit up for the best view, better still if there is a guitarist busking nearby. *Temple Lane South. www.walloffame.ie. Bus: All buses to Dame St or Wellington Quay.*

⑪ Irish Film Institute (IFI). A film buff's haven, the spacious and relaxing bar restaurant serves tasty burgers, pasta, and pies at lunchtimes and evenings. Fantastic value. *IFI, 6 Eustace St, Temple Bar.* ☎ *01-679 5744. www.irishfilm.ie. $.* ●

2 The Best Special-Interest Tours

Dublin's **Heroes**

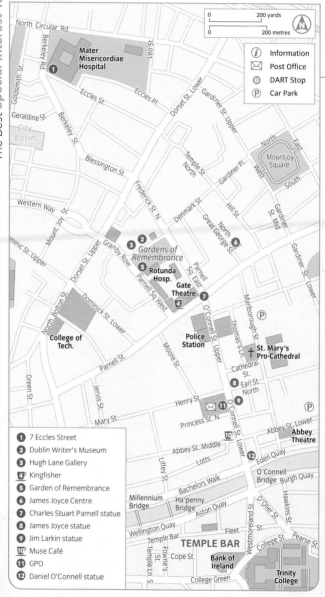

1. 7 Eccles Street
2. Dublin Writer's Museum
3. Hugh Lane Gallery
4. Kingfisher
5. Garden of Remembrance
6. James Joyce Centre
7. Charles Stuart Parnell statue
8. James Joyce statue
9. Jim Larkin statue
10. Muse Café
11. GPO
12. Daniel O'Connell statue

Dublin is renowned for its heroes, an endless list comprising political and creative heroes who shaped today's Dublin. This tour around O'Connell Street is a condensed area to give you a flavor of both, but you'll doubtless find countless more places of interest throughout the city during your stay. Heroes are celebrated in the form of attractive statues and sculptures dotted around.

START: **Bus 11, 13 & 16 to Eccles St.**

Dublin Writer's Museum.

❶ ★ No. 7 Eccles Street. In a city famous for literature, our first stop is, appropriately, the home of a fictional character: Leopold Bloom was the hero of James Joyce's epic *Ulysses*, a tale of "an ordinary day" in his life on June 16, a date now celebrated on Bloomsday (*see p 162*). The house itself was knocked down to build Mater Hospital, but a Blue Plaque with Joyce's portrait indicates the site of Bloom's home, with an excerpt from the book. The original door from No 7 is at the James Joyce Centre (see p 24) ⏱ *10 min.*

❷ ★ Dublin Writers' Museum. This is your best chance to get an insight into the lives of great Dublin writers all under one roof, telling the story of 300 years of great Irish literature. Quirky memorabilia include a colorful postcard from LA written by Brendan Behan, Samuel Beckett's telephone, letters from Yeats, early editions of *Waiting for Godot* and *Dracula*, and nuggets of info such as Oscar Wilde's boxing prowess. Great sculptures and portraits on the top floor include a noble Jonathan Swift and a more contemporary Christy Brown. ⏱ *1 hr. 18 Parnell Square,* ☎ *01-872 2077. www.writers museum.com. Admission: €7.70 adults, €6.60 concs, €4.80 children. Mon–Sat 10am–5pm; Sun & p/hols 11am–5pm. Jun, Jul & Aug Mon–Fri 10am–6pm.*

❸ ★★ Hugh Lane Gallery. Sir Hugh Lane, the founder of this gallery (*see p 22, bullet* ❸) containing art from Ireland and further afield, was a fascinating hero. He fulfilled his long desire to open a Dublin modern art gallery, persuading leading artists to donate pieces. It opened in 1908 in Harcourt Street, but Lane himself was killed on board the *RMS Lusitania*, which sank after being hit by a German torpedo. A dispute followed with London's National Gallery over the rightful home of the paintings, because Lane had changed his will without it being witnessed. Happily a compromise was eventually reached. Don't forget to visit the chaotically messy recreated studio of Dublin-born Francis Bacon. ⏱ 1 hr. Charlemont House, Parnell Square North. ☎ 01-222 5550. www.hughlane.ie. Free admission. Tue–Thur 10am–6pm, Fri & Sat 10am–5pm, Sun 11am–5pm. Guided tours: Tues 11am & Sun 1.30pm. Audiotours: €3.

4 ★★ **Kingfisher.** Choose from fresh fish and chips or full Irish breakfast with charming hospitality, popular with locals and builders. 166 Parnell St. ☎ 01-872 8732. $.

5 ★ **Garden of Remembrance.** Before hitting the busy O'Connell Street, take time out to relax in the peaceful garden. Opened in 1966, it commemorates the 50th anniversary of the Easter Rising and all those who died during the struggle for Irish freedom. The huge water feature is in the shape of a cross, at the far end of which is a huge sculpture by Oisin Kelly, based on the theme of the Children of Lir, its birds in flight symbolizing rebirth and resurrection. ⏱ 30 min. East Parnell Square.

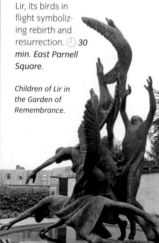

Children of Lir in the Garden of Remembrance.

6 ★★ **James Joyce Centre.** If you've ever wondered about the appeal of Joyce, and never quite got your head around his "stream of consciousness" method of writing (I plead guilty to that), here's a chance at least to learn about his life. The top floor is especially interesting, recreating the room in his studies in Trieste, Zurich, and Paris where he wrote Ulysses from 1914 to 1922. In fact, Joyce spent most of his life in exile. Difficult to believe that this much-lauded writer was at the time rejected by the Irish, who said he was "politically incorrect" in his criticism of the middle-class Catholic establishment. ⏱ 1 hr. 35 North Great George's St. ☎ 01-878 8547. www.jamesjoyce.ie. Admission: €5 adults, €4 concs. Tues–Sat 10am–5pm.

7 ★ **Charles Stuart Parnell statue.** The bronze statue of Parnell, born to a wealthy Protestant landowner in 1846, stands imposing at the top of O'Connell Street. After being elected to Parliament in 1878, he opposed the Irish land laws and became the accepted leader of the Irish nationalist movement. He advocated a boycott to influence landlords, and was sent to Kilmainham jail for his efforts. After release he joined the Liberal Party, which successfully introduced the first Irish Home Rule Bill. Sadly Parnell's reputation was ruined when his long-standing affair with Kitty O'Shea (with whom he had 3 children) surfaced when her husband filed for divorce. ⏱ 10 min. Corner of Upper O'Connell St & Parnell St.

8 ★ **James Joyce Statue.** By now you'll have read the book, viewed the study, and seen this hero's door. Now you can get a feeling what JJ looked like. This life-size sculpture stands at a busy pedestrianized street, with his characteristic nonchalant stance. He leans on his cane, provoking the unflattering nickname "the Prick with the Stick". Corner O'Connell St & North Earl St.

Parnell, who fell from grace.

9 ★ **Jim Larkin statue.** Created by Oisin Kelly (*see bullet **5**, Garden of Remembrance*), this is a real heroic posture: With arms outstretched, you can almost hear "Big Jim" rallying the troops, as he stands between the GPO and Cleary's. Liverpool-born Larkin (1874–1947) founded the Irish Transport & General Workers Union. This strong union threatened the bosses and members were forced to leave, leading to the great lock-out of 1913 when 100,000 workers were sacked. The struggle continued for eight months. The feisty Scouser was the first leader of the Irish Labour Party and continued his campaigning for some of Ireland's poorest workers. *O'Connell St, between Clery's & GPO.*

10 **kids** **Muse Café.** With your newly purchased books on Dublin's history and literature, take a coffee break on the 3rd-floor café at Eason bookstore. Try a comfy sofa or a window seat to peer at busy O'Connell Street below. *Eason, 40 Lower O'Connell St.* ☎ *01-858 3800. $.*

James Joyce observing North Earl Street.

11 ★★ **General Post Office.** Probably one of the most politically significant post offices in the world, this was the focal point of the Easter Rising of 1916. The Irish Volunteers and Irish Citizen Army seized the building on Easter Monday—a day when many British troops were at the horse-racing in Fairyhouse. On these very steps, just before midday, the Proclamation of Independence was read by Padraig Pearse. The rebels then remained inside for a week, until forced out by shelling from the British. One of the few remaining copies of the Declaration is on display inside the Philatelic Shop, to the right of the entrance. Visit the fascinating exhibition here, profiling the main characters involved in this political change. A sculpture of legendary Irish warrior Cuchulainn sits in the main window visible from the street. Poke your finger in the pillars' bullet holes outside—apparently it brings good luck. *An Post, O'Connell St. Counters open Mon–Sat 8am–8pm.*

12 ★★ **Daniel O'Connell statue.** Coming from a Catholic background in early 19th-century Dublin, O'Connell became a self-taught lawyer and politician, using his huge knowledge, influence, and political beliefs to change the life of Irish Catholics for good. Before then, they were forbidden to vote, study, join professions, or stand for parliament. Advocating non-violent political reform, he was committed to the Catholic emancipation movement and formed the Catholic Association in 1823. A year after winning election to the British Parliament—yet unable to take a seat because of his religion—the Catholic Emancipation Act was passed, making O'Connell the uncrowned king of Ireland in many people's eyes. As befits his status, his statue stands at one of the most visible parts of the city. *O'Connell St.*

Dublin **with Kids**

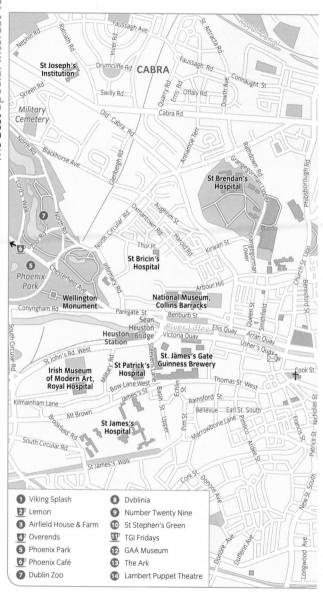

1. Viking Splash
2. Lemon
3. Airfield House & Farm
4. Overends
5. Phoenix Park
6. Phoenix Café
7. Dublin Zoo
8. Dvblinia
9. Number Twenty Nine
10. St Stephen's Green
11. TGI Fridays
12. GAA Museum
13. The Ark
14. Lambert Puppet Theatre

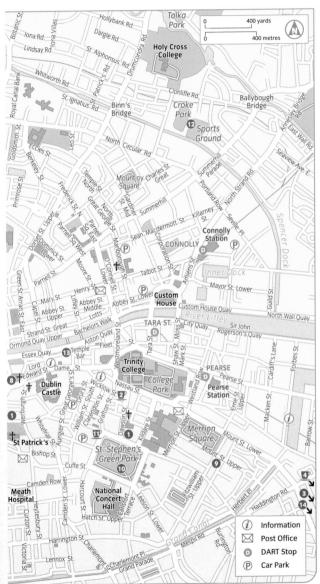

ℹ️	Information
✉️	Post Office
Ⓓ	DART Stop
Ⓟ	Car Park

Small is beautiful, like many of the attractions listed below that I consider to be tailor-made for kids. Don't think of attempting to do all these in a day—it would exhaust the hardiest of adults! Instead, pick places and tours suitable for your children's ages and interests. For a relaxing time out, the outdoor spaces are brilliant (even without sunshine!) and don't forget the larger galleries: the National Museum of Archeology (see p 41) and Collins Barracks (see p 57) will keep little ones amused, and even the National Gallery (see p 13) has children's activity packs available. A day trip to the coast is always a winner with all ages (see p 147).

① ★ **Viking Splash.** A sure hit with kids, this entertaining tour by land and sea led by a costumed guide gives an amusing take on the city, touching on its Viking history and also pointing out historic highlights. Traveling on a "Duck"—a seven-tonne amphibious World War II tank—kids (and adults if they wish) get to wear Viking helmets and roar at passers-by. Endure the inevitable squeals as the tank then launches into the water for a tour around the docklands. This tour is on the pricey side for adults. ⏱ *80 min. Pick-up points cnr Merrion Row & Dawson St, and cnr Patrick St & Bull Alley. Reservations recommended:* ☎ *01-707 6000. Daily every 2 hrs 10am–5pm. €20 adults, €10 children. Bus: All buses to Stephen's Green, or 49, 50, 51B & 77 for Patrick St.*

② **Lemon.** Pancakes and waffles galore, both savory and sweet, from this cheerful orange café. The ice-cream banana supreme crepe makes a great late morning snack. *66 South William St.* ☎ *01-672 9044. $.*

③ ★★ **Airfield House & Farm.** In the mid-town suburb of Dundrum, this gorgeous farm cottage built in the 1820s has been updated as an urban farm, with livestock, ornate gardens, a small museum, and a wonderful café. A good all-weather option, there are year-round activities plus opportunities to "meet" the goats, geese, and cows (and you don't have to be a child to enjoy that), picnic in the flower-filled grounds, or take a guided walk. Within the

Ford at Airfield Trust Car Museum.

grounds, the tiny Car Museum has vintage vehicles belonging to two feisty sisters who lived in the house, including a 1923 Peugeot and 1927 Rolls Royce. ⏱ *2–4 hr. Upper Kilmacud Rd, Dundrum.* ☎ *01-298 4301. www.airfield.ie. €6 adults, €3 children, €18 family. Tue–Sat 10am–5pm; Sun & hols 11am–5pm. Luas: Balally.*

④ **Overends** Visitors to Airfield House will be glad of this charming café inside the Visitors Centre, with tasty buffet and snacks. Very popular with local mums. *Upper Kilmacud Rd, Dundrum.* ☎ *01-298 4301. $.*

⑤ ★★★ **Phoenix Park.** The largest enclosed park in a European capital, this covers a mammoth 700 hectares (1730 acres). Possible but tiring to walk the whole park, there are highlights for children: The **Visitors Centre** near Ashtown Gate has a lovely exhibition of the park's history through the ages, displays on the Viking grave discovered here, and an interactive wildlife section for younger kids. **Bicycle Hire** is inside the Parkgate Street main entrance, including child-sized, tandems and baby-carriers, giving the best chance to explore the park in all its green glory. Bring a picnic and make the most of the space. *(See also p 92)* ⏱ *2–4 hr. Entrances on Parkfield St & Ashtown Gate.* ☎ *01-677 0095. Park: Free admission; open 24 hr. Visitors Centre: Mar–Sep: daily 10am–6pm; Oct–Feb: daily 10am–5pm. Bike hire daily 9.30am–5.30pm;* ☎ *01-679 1046. Luas: Museum (red line); Bus: 25, 51, 68 & 69.*

⑥ **Phoenix Café.** A huge outdoor courtyard will cater for all ages, with drinks, cakes, meals, and snacks. It's a great space to relax, and also has tasty takeaways. *Visitor's Centre, Phoenix Park, Ashtown Gate.* ☎ *01-677 0090. $.*

⑦ ★ **Dublin Zoo.** Located inside Phoenix Park, the zoo has come a long way since its origins in the 1830s, with few examples of wild beasts sitting sadly in cages (a blessing for animal lovers like myself). Dublin Zoo, like many others around the world, helps to breed endangered species, and recently created the African Plains section thanks to a 13-hectare (32-acre) extension given by the Government. Wander along the paths and try to spot a tiger, white rhino, or zebra, and go to the World of Primates to see the orangutan family, whose history reads like something from a soap opera. My personal favorites, the Big Cats, are hard to spot thanks to the space they are able to inhabit, which I guess is the flip side of decent living conditions. There are several daily "Meet the Keeper" sessions during summer; weekends only in winter. Pick a dry day to enjoy the leafy surroundings. ⏱ *2 hr. Phoenix Park,* ☎ *01-474 8900. www.dublinzoo.ie. Admission: €14 adults, €11 concs, €9.50 children 4–15, From €40 family.*

Cute baby gorilla at Dublin Zoo.

Open daily Mon–Sat from 9.30am, Sun from 10.30am. Closing time varies monthly; check in advance. Luas: Museum (red line); Bus: 37, 38 7 39. Luas: Museum (red line); Bus: 25, 51, 68 & 69.

⑧ ★★ Dublinia.

Viking gods at Dublinia.

Step back into a Viking era in the heart of medieval Dublin. Kids will love the recreated fairground with sound effects, medicine stalls (open the drawers to see the cures!), and the invitation to throw balls at the man in the stocks. Ogle at the 900-year-old creepy skeleton and a wolf skull—amazing to think that Dublin was forest-covered in the 15th century. The Viking World exhibition explains the history and mystery, including the origins of the swastika—a Viking good luck symbol long before the Nazis got hold of it. There's a section on the language of the runes where kids can make a rubbing of their name. If it's not raining, older ones can climb the 96 steps to the top of the viewing tower in the adjacent St Michael's Church for a panoramic view. ⏱ 1 hr. St Michael's Hill, Christchurch. ☎ 01-679 4611.

www.dublinia.ie. Admission: €6.25 adults, €5.25 concs, €3.75 children, €17 family. Apr–Sep: daily 10am–5pm; Oct–Mar: Mon–Fri 11am–4pm; Sat & Sun 10am-4pm. Bus: 50 & 78A.

⑨ ★ Number Twenty Nine.

This small house museum is a lovely insight into home life in Georgian Dublin. Children can get a feel for the era thanks to the colorful tour describing typical middle-class family life. Going from the basement up to the attic, the rooms have retained original artifacts from 1800. The nursery, tucked away at the top of the house, is a highlight with two early 19th-century doll's houses complete with miniature furniture. And of course no well-to-do family would be complete without a governess teaching them needlepoint. The elegant furnishings, mainly from the Georgian era or even earlier, include a handsome long-case clock in the hallway, ornate mahogany chairs, and a portrait of revolutionary Robert Emmet with a mysterious history. ⏱ 1 hr. 29 Fitzwilliam St Lower, ☎ 01-702 6165. www.esc.ie/no29. Admission: €5 adults, €2.50 concs, free under 16. Tue–Sat 10am–5pm, Sun 1pm–5pm. Closed Mon & hols. Bus: 7, 10 & 45.

Nursery at Number Twenty Nine Museum.

10 ★ St Stephen's Green. The expanse of green is a must for young kids to run around. And I have yet to see an adult who doesn't enjoy feeding the ducks: wander to the pond, which is to the left of the Fusiliers' Arch entrance, and dispense with your leftover sandwiches. There's also a children's playground near the center of the green. It's easy to see how this was once prime pram-pushing territory back in Georgian times, such are the lovely willows, flower-beds, and the general feeling of a green oasis. During summer, the occasional free play is performed in the amphitheater, and music played in the bandstand at lunchtimes. ⏱ *1 hr. Main entrance crn West St Stephen's Green & South King St. Luas: St Stephen's Green.*

11 TGI Fridays. When only a burger, pizza, or ice cream will do, this branch will satisfy a monster appetite. Coloring books and crayons keep little visitors entertained. *St Stephen's Green West (also accessed via Stephen's Green Shopping Centre).* ☎ *01-478 1233. $$.*

12 ★★ GAA Museum. Any kid who loves football, or fans of any sport, will love the challenge of trying to hit the ball with the hurley (like a polo stick) or kick the Gaelic football over the posts. Many of the exhibits are interactive. The stadium tour is a real buzz and the novelty of standing on the pitch in a huge stadium with a capacity of nearly 90,000 gets any spine tingling. ⏱ *90 min. See p 17 for info.*

13 ★ The Ark. Europe's first purpose-built cultural center for children has exhibitions, performances, and workshops. A fun, bright venue, this is chock-full of entertainment, and for any given event a suggested age range is specified. During the summer, there are performances most days that might be music, story-telling, or drama-related. Tucked away in Temple Bar, this former Presbyterian Meeting House (1728) houses an indoor theater, an outdoor amphitheater, gallery spaces, and a workshop. *11a Eustace St, Temple Bar.* ☎ *01-670 6788. www.ark.ie. Bus: All buses via Dame St.*

14 ★ Lambert Puppet Theatre. More than just Punch and Judy: take a trip to the seaside for shows every weekend throughout the year, usually of popular fairy stories with the occasional Oscar Wilde children's tale thrown in. For the last 35 years, all the puppets have been hand-made on site by the Lambert family. The theater is also the venue for September's International Puppet Festival. After the show, take the kids upstairs to the museum's permanent collection of puppets past and present from around the world. Shows are suitable mainly for kids aged 4–9, although adults may secretly enjoy it even more. *Clifton Lane, Monkstown,* ☎ *01-280 0974. www. lambertpuppettheatre.com. Shows every Sat & Sun 3.30pm, 90 min. Telephone booking advised. DART: Monkstown.*

Floral delights at Stephen's Green.

Georgian **Dublin**

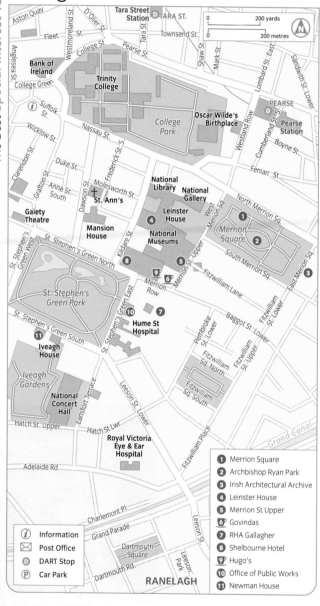

1	Merrion Square
2	Archbishop Ryan Park
3	Irish Architectural Archive
4	Leinster House
5	Merrion St Upper
6	Govindas
7	RHA Gallagher
8	Shelbourne Hotel
9	Hugo's
10	Office of Public Works
11	Newman House

Map labels:
Aston Quay, D'Olier St., Tara Street Station, TARA ST., Fleet St., Westmoreland St., College St., Townsend St., Shaw St., Mark St., Sandwith St. Lower, Lombard St. East, Anglesea St., Pearse St., Bank of Ireland, College Green, Trinity College, College Park, Oscar Wilde's Birthplace, Westland Row, Cumberland St. S., PEARSE, Pearse Station, Boyne St., Suffolk St., College Green, Wicklow St., Nassau St., North Merrion Sq., Fenian St., Chic-arendon St., Duke St., Frederick St. S., Molesworth St., National Library, National Gallery, Merrion Sq. West, Grafton St., Anne St. South, Dawson St., St. Ann's, Leinster House, Gaiety Theatre, Mansion House, National Museums, Merrion Square, South Merrion Sq., East Merrion Sq., St. Stephen's Green West, St. Stephen's Green North, Kildare St., Merrion St. Upper, Fitzwilliam Lane, Merrion Row, St. Stephen's Green Park, St. Stephen's Green East, Hume St Hospital, Pembroke St. Lower, Baggot St. Lower, Fitzwilliam St. Lower, Fitzwilliam St. Upper, Iveagh House, St. Stephen's Green South, Iveagh Gardens, National Concert Hall, Earlsfort Terrace, Leeson St. Lower, Fitzwilliam Sq. North, Fitzwilliam Sq. South, Hatch St. Upper, Hatch St Lwr, Royal Victoria Eye & Ear Hospital, Fitzwilliam Place, Grand Canal, Adelaide Rd., Charlemont Pl., Grand Parade, Leeson St., Dartmouth Square, Leeson Park, Dartmouth Rd., RANELAGH

Scale: 0 – 200 yards / 0 – 200 metres

Legend:
- (i) Information
- ✉ Post Office
- Ⓓ DART Stop
- Ⓟ Car Park

Graceful Georgian architecture has long been a major landmark of Dublin. Flat-fronted five-storey rows became part of the cityscape from the 1700s, when developers opted for Georgian-style squares that would house the aristocracy and affluent gentry. Although the Northside saw the first such developments, it was the Southside that was always seen as the location "to be", especially around Merrion Square, explored on this walk. The man to thank for the mushrooming Georgian fad was the Earl of Kildare, who located his new mansion here when the area was just boggy farmland. How times have changed. START: **Bus 4, 5, 7 & 45 to Merrion Square.**

Typical Georgian doorway.

❶ ★ **Merrion Square.** The most famous and least altered of Dublin's Georgian squares, this was completed at the end of the 18th century and many buildings contain their original features. It's also a square of blue plaques galore: look out for the childhood home of Oscar Wilde at no. 1, the most prestigious address and now the American College, the home of Daniel O'Connell at no. 58, and William Butler Yeats at no. 82. Here you can see the ornate fanlights; the semi-circular glass above the doorway was more ornate to denote the wealth of the owners. Doorways were typically wide to accommodate the wide bustles of the lady's Georgian dresses. Doors are typically colorful here: local

folklore has it that after Queen Victoria died and the British painted their doors black for mourning, the Irish painted theirs anything but!

❷ kids ★ **Archbishop Ryan Park.** Inside Merrion Square, this small public park is a lovely green space with lawns and neat meandering pathways. Dotted around the park are several worthy statues, including the slouching pose of Oscar Wilde, with each color of the sculpture made from a different natural stone. Wearing the college tie of Trinity College, his expression is half humorous and half serious conveying both sides of his writing and life. There is also a bust of Michael Collins, and a huge sculpture of a wooden jester's chair dedicated to Dermot Morgan, star of the TV series "Father Ted". ⏱ **45 min.**

Michael Collins in Archbishop Ryan Park.

❸ ★ **Irish Architectural Archive.** The largest of the terraced houses on Merrion Square, this is one of the few archives with public access. Browse through photos from the 1930s and drawings from the 1700s of houses throughout Ireland (hint: pick a street in Dublin that you've just visited to discover its history). I was able to see old photos of my grandparent's house. The small gallery hosts interesting photography exhibitions, and usually free lunchtime lectures to accompany them (booking essential). ⏱ *45 min. 45 Merrion Square,* ☎ *01-6633 040. www.iarc.ie. Free admission. Tue–Fri 10am–5pm.*

④ ★ Leinster House. Walk up Merrion Square South and peek through the huge railings on Merrion Street to the two houses of the National Parliament: the Dáil (House of Deputies) and Seanad (Senate). Built in 1745 as a townhouse for the Earl of Kildare, who later became the Duke of Leinster, this is said to be the prototype for the US White House (built by Dublin-educated architect James Hoban). At the time, the area was undeveloped and known rather disparagingly as "the lands of tib and tom". The Earl was advised against building a townhouse in the "country". However he had the last laugh when two decades later, this was the most fashionable part of town. Take a tour of the Department of the Taoiseach (Prime Minister) on Saturdays, with the privileged view of the PM's office including family photos and a beautiful Bossi fireplace, meeting rooms, stained glass, and wonderful artwork adorning the walls, all by local artists. ⏱ *tour 1 hr, Sat every hour 10.30–1.30pm; tickets from National Gallery from 10am.* ☎ *01-619 4000. Meet inside Merrion St entrance.*

⑤ ★ Merrion Street Upper. From Leinster House you'll pass the wonderful **Museum of Natural History** (known locally as the "dead zoo"), which will hopefully be open by 2009 after restoration. **Number 24 Merrion Street Upper** was the birthplace of Arthur Wellesley, better known as the first Duke of Wellington.

His parents were Anglo-Irish ascendancy and he kept in contact with his Irish friends and family despite becoming one of England's greatest military leaders. When someone told him that being born in Dublin made him Irish, he allegedly replied "Being born in a stable does not make one a horse". His home is now part of the elegant **Merrion Hotel** (see p 144), superbly restored and famous for its artwork as well as its luxury rooms. On the right is the tiny **Huguenot Cemetery** (now closed), resting place for the French Protestants expelled from France in the 17th century.

⑥ 🧒 Govindas. Simple Indian vegetarian joint run by Hari Krishnas, but no orange robes here. A choice of dishes is served with rice, for cheap filling lunch specials or takeaways. *18 Merrion Row.* ☎ *01-661 5095. $.*

⑦ ★★ RHA Gallagher. *Due to major renovations, the gallery will reopen in September 2008.* Although this gallery has little to do with Georgian history, it's in the area, which is reason enough for a visit. The Royal Hibernian Academy has been an artist-based institution since 1823.

Leinster House forms a majestic landmark.

Historic hospitality at The Shelbourne.

The spacious gallery, much newer, showcases contemporary artists mainly from Ireland. There's also a small section for young upcoming artists, making this gallery good for trying to spot future greats. Sculpture is mainly on the 1st floor, with photography, oils, and prints throughout. New additions include a café and bookstore. ⏲ *45 min. Ely Place.* ☎ *01-661 2558. www.royalhibernian academy.ie. Free admission. Tue–Sat 11am–5pm; Thur 11am–8pm; Sun 2–5pm.*

⑧ ★ Shelbourne Hotel. Dublin's most celebrated hotel has enjoyed a colorful past. A Georgian masterpiece founded in 1824 and named after the Earl of Shelbourne, it has hosted the great and the good in Irish high society, and visitors like Orson Welles and William Thackeray. Take tea in the lounge to the dulcet tones of the grand piano and think back to the Easter Rising in 1916, when a British machine-gun crew positioned themselves on the 5th floor. Ladies taking tea were advised to move to a back room, advice they heeded quickly when one of the noble tea-takers had a bullet fly through her hat and hit a mirror at the back. The hotel was also the venue for the meeting to draft the Irish Constitution in 1922. Pop in for afternoon tea if you fancy splashing out. *27 St Stephen's Green.* ☎ *01-663 4500. www.theshelbourne.ie.*

⑨ Hugo's. Stylish, comfortable restaurant and wine bar serving a tempting charcuterie or cheese platter, ideal for sharing a late lunch. Brunch is also served during weekends until 4pm. *6 Merrion Row.* ☎ *01-676 5955. $$.*

⑩ ★ Office of Public Works. Pop into this beautiful Georgian building for the exhibition of marble on the walls of the entrance foyer. Over 40 different types of Irish marble are displayed in panels, a rainbow of colors including the gorgeous green from Connemara, black speckled with white shapes looking like a night sky from Galway, and rust red from Clonony. Take the chance to admire the ornate interior. ⏲ *30 min. 51 St Stephen's Green.* ☎ *01-647 6000. Mon–Thur 9.15am–5.30pm, Fri 9.15pm–5.15pm.*

⑪ ★★ Newman House. Here's another Georgian gem. Best known for its exquisite 18th-century stuccowork by the Lafrancini brothers, this was originally two separate houses, joined together in the mid-19th century to form the Catholic University (now UCD). It's named after its founder John Henry Newman. Famous ex-pupils include Jesuit poet Gerard Manley Hopkins and James Joyce. (If you've read *Portrait of the Artist* you might recognize his description of the Physics Theatre.) Highlight is the Apollo Room, with plasterwork scenes of Apollo and the nine muses of the arts. Shift your gaze from the ceilings to the magnificent Cuban mahogany staircase as you sweep down; no wonder that the film *Becoming Jane* about the steamy life of Jane Austen, was filmed here. *85–86 St Stephen Green.* ☎ *01-716 7422. Entry by tour only. Admission: €5 adults; €4 concs. June–Aug, Tues–Fri, 2, 3 & 4pm.*

Trinity College

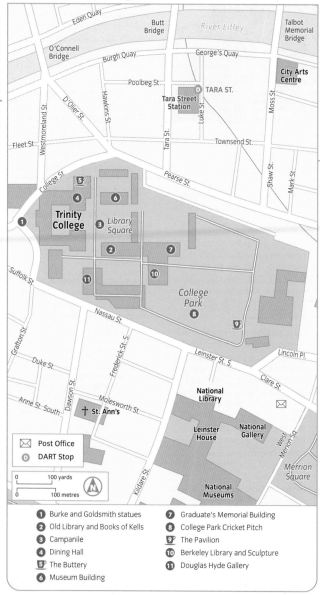

1. Burke and Goldsmith statues
2. Old Library and Books of Kells
3. Campanile
4. Dining Hall
5. The Buttery
6. Museum Building
7. Graduate's Memorial Building
8. College Park Cricket Pitch
9. The Pavilion
10. Berkeley Library and Sculpture
11. Douglas Hyde Gallery

With a history stretching back to 1592, Ireland's oldest college has seen wonderful writers and esteemed academics graduate from its hallowed halls. Set up in Tudor times by Queen Elizabeth I, Catholics were forbidden to join unless they accepted the Protestant faith. Astoundingly, these restrictions were not completely lifted until 1970; 70% of today's students are Catholics. Covering a vast 16 hectares (40 acres), this oasis of cobbled and sculpture-filled green lies calmly in the city center. Join the crowds to gaze at the amazing Book of Kells, then hang out among some of Dublin's brainiest, although not everyone has been so complimentary about Trinity's educational excellence: ex-student Samuel Beckett allegedly quipped "Trinity's graduates were like cream: thick and rich."

START: Bus 15, 50 & 77 to College Street.

Trinity old boy Oliver Goldsmith.

❶ Burke and Goldsmith statues. Guarding the Regent House entrance to Trinity are the imposing statues of Edmund Burke and Oliver Goldsmith, cast in white marble by 19th-century sculptor John Henry Foley. Burke (1729–1797) became a British statesman thanks to his prowess in political philosophy. Author of *She Stoops to Conquer*, Goldsmith (1728–1774) had a colorful life after graduating in theology and law from Trinity; he studied medicine in Edinburgh and traveled through Europe before becoming a noted poet and playwright.

❷ Old Library & Book of Kells. Inside the grand Old Library, a huge paneled hall containing more than 200,000 books, visitors line up around the block for this one. The illuminated copy of the Book of Kells, four gospels written in Latin around AD 800, is lavishly decorated and one of the most famous books in the world. Two volumes are displayed in glass cases and, as part of the complete *Turning Darkness into Light* exhibition, also on display are the Book of Armagh and the even older Book of Durrow. If, like me, you dislike peering through crowds for a glimpse (I'm too short!), visit around 1pm when it's not quite as busy. Even if it's hard to get a proper look at the Book, the view down the length of the Old Library is quite a sight.

❸ Campanile. The most striking and famous monument inside the Trinity grounds, the white Campanile or belltower grabs your attention as you enter through the main archway. It dates back to the mid-19th century and was built by Sir Charles Lanyon. The tower stands on the site of the college's original foundations, from 400 years earlier. Walk all the way around and gaze up at its peak—it looks even better in sunshine.

❹ Dining Hall. This may not be open for visitors once The Buttery (the restaurant for visitors) reopens downstairs in 2008, but there has been talk of it opening during the summer. If so, you have a treat in

The Campanile

store: The incredibly high-ceilinged interior and the wooden paneling make even a cup of tea and scone seem special. The building was originally designed by Richard Castle in the 1740s, but after collapsing twice, was rebuilt by Hugh Darley around 1760. Damaged yet again, this time by fire in 1984, it underwent prize-winning restoration.

5 ★ **The Buttery.** Reopened in September 2007 after major restoration, the Buttery has long been a popular eating spot for visitors to Trinity College, and students in holiday time. *Trinity College.* ☎ *01-896 1000. $.*

6 **Graduate's Memorial Building.** The GMB now houses student accommodation—streets ahead of the sort I had to endure—and is also home to the university's history and philosophical societies. The neo-Gothic Victorian building was designed by Sir Thomas Drew in 1892, one of 19th-century Ireland's most distinguished architects. It's not possible to enter, but walk around the outside and peer at some of the detailed stonework.

7 **Museum Building.** Home to the geography and geology departments, this is one of my favorite Dublin hidden gems. Designed by architects Dean and Woodward, with stonemasonry by the famed O'Shea brothers, it was built in the mid-19th century with a combination of Byzantine and Moorish influences. Samuel Haughton, inventor of the "humane hangman's drop" was professor here in the late 19th century. On entering the main door, two huge skeletons of giant Irish deer peer down. Walk through and look up to the domed ceiling and the green marbled banisters. The 3rd floor's tiny Geology Museum is a must for fans of meteorites, fossils, and early amphibians, where Patrick, the friendly curator, is happy to allow visitors to look around. Scenes from British 1985 film *Educating Rita* were shot here. *Geology Museum.* ☎ *01-896 1477. Mon–Fri 10am–5pm. Free admission.*

8 **College Park cricket pitch.** To cricket fans like me, it's always a pleasure to see a match at the Dublin University Cricket Club, stalwart of Irish cricket for nearly 200 years, and playing here since the 1820s. Most matches take place at weekends between May and early September, and when the weather is fine students and locals sprawl out on the grass around the boundary. It's fair to say that few would follow every ball being bowled, although since Ireland shocked the world when they beat Pakistan in the 2007 Cricket World Cup, the interest in the sport has grown.

Trinity College: Practical matters

Be prepared for a long queue for the Book of Kells at most times, with occasional temporary closure for visiting foreign dignitaries. It's worthwhile buying a combined ticket for a guided walk of Trinity, given by a student, including entrance to the Book of Kells, for just an extra couple of euros. Admission to the Book of Kells is €8 adults, €7 concs, €16 family. Children under 12 free. Open: Mon–Sat 9.30am–7pm, Sun (May–Sep) 9.30am–4.30pm, Sun (Oct–Apr) noon–4.30pm. Combined Book of Kells and campus tour: €10. Tours: daily 10.15am, 10.55am–3.40pm (every 40 mins).

9 ★ **The Pavilion.** At the eastern end of the cricket pitch is "the Pav". At weekends during a cricket match beer might run out quickly, so be quick to stock up on drinks. ☎ *01-896 1000. $.*

10 Berkeley Library and sculpture. Some love it and most hate it (I fall into the latter), and the library's position between two architectural masterpieces has caused controversy since day one. Designed by Paul Koralek, it honors Bishop George Berkeley, famed for his philosophical theory of "immaterialism" (things that can't be proved cannot exist), which went against the theories of Sir Isaac Newton and the Catholic Church. On his world travels during the early 1700s, he argued for creating universities for the "natives" and although this didn't succeed in his lifetime, a university was eventually set up in California in his name. (In the USA it's pronounced "Barkeley"). Arnaldo Pomodoro's gleaming sculpture, "Sphere with Sphere" (1983), stands outside the library.

11 Douglas Hyde Gallery. Housed in the 1970s-built **Arts Building**, this gallery accommodates an eclectic collection. Housing only temporary exhibitions in two rooms, this includes work from top contemporary artists from Ireland and overseas, in a variety of media including Japanese textiles, nomadic bags and faces, and African masks and fetishes. Few people seem to wander through but it's worth a look. ☎ *01-896 1116. Free admission. Mon–Fri 11am–6pm; Sat 11am–4.45pm.*

Pomodoro's "Sphere within a Sphere" sculpture outside Berkeley Library.

Vikings and Medieval Dubh Linn

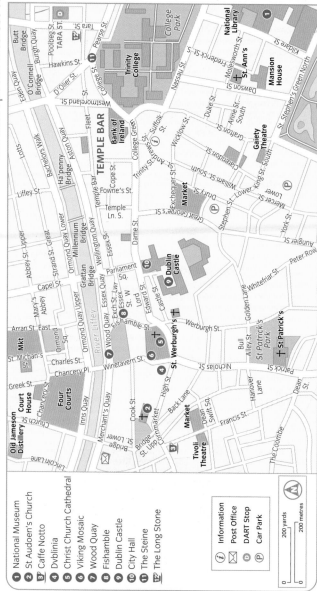

1 National Museum
2 St Audoen's Church
3 Caffe Notto
4 Dvblinia
5 Christ Church Cathedral
6 Viking Mosaic
7 Wood Quay
8 Fishamble
9 Dublin Castle
10 City Hall
11 The Steine
12 The Long Stone

ⓘ Information
⊠ Post Office
Ⓓ DART Stop
Ⓟ Car Park

0   200 yards
0   200 metres

Although visitors flock to Dublin for literary wonders and political history, its Viking past is a hidden treasure. Back in AD 837, two large fleets of Norsemen with scores of ships arrived on the Liffey and soon established a camp, known as An Dubh Linn (literally Black Pool) near Dublin Castle. Slave markets, plundering, and brisk trading soon followed. Today, there are remnants of those Viking and Medieval days, especially around Temple Bar, Wood Quay, and Dublin Castle, with so much more underground. Dublin Corporation seized on the date of AD 998, which was thought to be the year when Norse King Glun Iariann agreed to pay taxes, seen as a huge landmark in Dublin's history and created "Dublin's Millennium" in 1998.

START: **Bus 7, 10, 11 & 13 to Merrion Row.**

1 ★★ National Museum. This great museum certainly knows how to pack archaeological eras into a small area (see p 40, bullet 1). Highlights from the Viking section include relics discovered in the 1960s and 1970s from Wood Quay (see p 43), a huge urban excavation. Exhibits include domestic artifacts, and even weighing scales proving there was more to the Vikings than being warriors and pillagers; they were also traders and made Dublin a good base. From the cemeteries unearthed in the Dublin areas of Kilmainham and Islandbridge—the largest outside Scandinavia—you'll see the skeletal remains and weapons they were buried with. Public tours are given at 11.30am and 3pm daily. *See p 9 for details.*

2 ★★★ St Audoen's Church. Here's one place to turn back several centuries: Dublin's only medieval parish church is located on what was the principal street and was completed in 1212, although a grave slab 300 years older indicates that an earlier church occupied the same site. An exhibition inside the **Visitor's Centre** illustrates the area during medieval times, as the city's commercial heart. The church itself

The Portlester tomb.

is more impressive (ask the staff to show you around). Look out for the 1190 baptismal font and the funerary tomb of a 1620 Alderman, decorated with skull and crossbones (proving that it didn't always symbolize poison or pirates). In the tower, the 15th-century Portlester tomb has effigies of Baron Portlester and his wife Margaret looking exceedingly restful. Sunday services (Church of Ireland) are open to everyone, and are a perfect opportunity to hear Ireland's oldest bells, dating back to 1423. Opposite the main reception desk, I love the postcards of various tradesmen of the time, telling stories of their lives. ⏱ *45 min. Cornmarket, High St* ☎ *01-677 0088. May–Oct: (Season may extend from 2008). Free admission. 9.30pm–5.30pm daily.*

3 ★ **Caffè Notto.** The former bank has kept the brick-walled interior and now serves coffee sandwiches, and smoothies in relaxed surroundings. Locals love to peruse the daily papers, or pull up a stool to watch the busy Cornmarket outside, surrounded by the work of college artists on the walls. *79 Thomas St.* ☎ *01-454 7223. $*

4 kids ★ **Dvblinia and the Viking World.** One especially for the kids (see p 26, bullet **8**), the heritage center is aptly built at Dublin's medieval heart, illustrating local life since Strongbow and his knights captured the city in 1170. Check out the 3rd-floor museum, with artifacts from the Wood Quay (see p 43) excavations, including the skeleton of a 12th-century Hiberno-Norse woman—probably the only chance you have of looking a 900-year-old Dubliner in the eye. The top floor's Viking World has an

Christ Church's crypt.

interactive exhibition about the Scandinavian raiders, looting monasteries and worshiping pagan gods, yet also innovating trade and town development in Dublin and many other Irish cities. ⏱ *1 hr. See p 30 for details.*

5 kids ★ **Christ Church Cathedral.** Originally a wooden structure founded by the Norse King Sitric in the 11th century, the cathedral was replaced by a stone building and then, 700 years later, restored. Inside, look out for Strongbow's tomb, and some fabulous 13th-century original floor tiles. Descend to the medieval crypt, extending under the entire cathedral and dating back to the 11th century, making it Dublin's oldest structure. If you peep through the glass in the floor, you can see the 11th-century foundations, later demolished by the Anglo-Normans. There's also a taste of punishment, medieval style, with a pair of 17th-century stocks, which were originally in the churchyard. ⏱ *1 hr. See p 15 for details.*

6 ★ **Viking Mosaic.** Next to Christ Church Cathedral, on the southern end of Winetavern Street, look down at the pavement. In dark stone, you will see the full-sized plan of a typical early Viking building site.

While you're in the vicinity, keep a look out for bronze slabs in the pavement, including one outside the main entrance to Christ Church Cathedral, indicating the locations of artifacts excavated. You can see the real things in the National Museum (see p 9). *Winetavern St.*

7 kids ★ **Wood Quay.** Scene of the city's most controversial construction: as Dublin Corporation started building their new HQ here in the 1970s, preserved remains of the Viking city and medieval city walls were revealed, which turned out to be one of Europe's most important Viking sites. When the council showed no intention of changing their plans, locals protested en masse. After court cases, huge public campaigns—known as the Battle of Wood Quay—and further excavations, the building plans were altered, leaving the remains of the city walls piled up in the basement and the Viking relics in the National Museum. When the last phase of the construction was completed in the 1990s, the site was built over. A symbolic representation of the era, the **Viking ship sculpture** by Betty Maguire, is adjacent to the much-hated council offices. *Viking ship by Wood Quay, between O'Donovan Rossa and Grattan bridges.*

8 ★ **Fishamble.** Although filled with modern-day hedonistic temples of pleasure and culture (pubs and clubs), this is the heart of medieval Dublin and a few relics still remain. **Fishamble Street** is the oldest street, original location of the fish market. Look out for the plaque on the wall next to the George Frederic Handel Hotel (no. 16–18), marking the spot of the former "Musick Hall", venue for the world's first performance of Handel's Messiah— which he also conducted—on April 13 1742. Look for the Turk's Head bar on **Essex Gate**: Outside that, and the Czech Inn (formerly Isolde's Tower) opposite, are two stone pillars marking the original city gates.

9 ★★ **Dublin Castle.** The tour of the castle interior gives a flavor of the high life of royalty and the political elite. But the outside has an older history. Several years after 60 Viking warships sailed up the Liffey in AD 837, the castle was the site of a high-ridged fort. After the Irish expelled them, the Norsemen returned and settled just west of the castle, building up a town called Dyflinn with the King's palace on the site of the castle. The site of the original "black pool" (from where the name Dyflinn and later Dubh Linn originate) is the roughly circular garden behind the

The site of the original "black pool" can be found in the garden of Dublin Castle.

Viking landmark in the midst of traffic.

castle. If you take the castle tour, you'll visit the Undercroft, where parts of the town defenses and settlements can be seen. ⏱ *1 hr. See p 14 for details.*

⑩ ★ **City Hall.** If you haven't yet ventured beyond the City Hall's stunning atrium, wander to the basement's **Story of the Capital** exhibition, which gives a decent insight to the city at the time of the Vikings, but more interesting are the relics from Medieval times. Look out for the original 13th-century City Seal, made from two bronze moulds, which were filled with hot red liquid wax and sealed onto legal documents. There is also the earliest Norman document in Ireland, dating back to 1171. (see p 40, bullet ⑩). ⏱ *30 min. Cork Hill, Dame St* ☎ *01-222 2204. Admission: €4 adults, €1.50 children. Mon–Sat 10am–5.15pm, Sun 2–5pm.*

⑪ ★ **The Steine.** As the traffic roars around you in probably Dublin's busiest roundabout, it's hard to believe that The Steine in the center marks the area where the Vikings first landed. This granite slab represents the original Standing Stones, 360–420cm (12–14 feet) high, that the Vikings erected in the 10th or 11th centuries to mark the boundaries of their Dublin territories. This one is a reproduction, carved by Cliodna Cussen, and depicts the faces of Ivor, the 9th-century Viking King of Dublin. In front is the Townsend Street police station, once the headquarters of the Garda and where Michael Collins entered secretly during the 1916 uprising to take a peak at the records. *Junction of D'Olier, Townsend & College Streets.*

⑫ ★★ **The Long Stone.** With timber window-frames, a small stained-glass skylight, and wonderful carved wooden ceiling, this pub's theme fits well into the area's history. Looking more like a Medieval museum, its centerpiece is the fireplace surround—a mesmerizing sculpture of Balder, the Viking god of light and warmth. Get back to practical matters; have a drink, with excellent food served all day. *10 Townsend St.* ☎ *01-671 8102. $.* ●

Balder, Viking god of light and warmth.

North of the **Royal Canal**

1. Botanic Gardens
2. Garden Catering
3. Pyramid Church
4. Glasnevin Cemetery
5. Gravediggers Pub
6. Royal Canal
7. Brendan Behan Sculpture
8. GAA Museum
9. Mountjoy Square

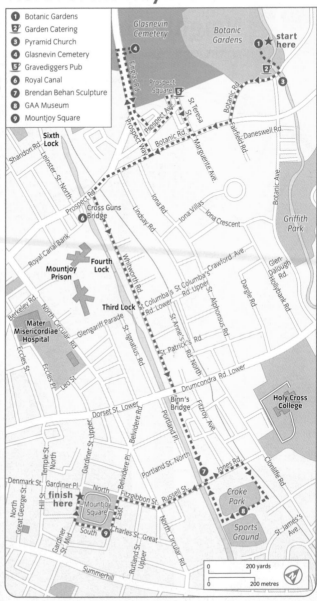

Off the beaten track, this northern walk encompasses some of my favorites, with gardens, heroic history, peaceful locks, sporting prowess, and a most unusual church. Try and save this tour for a fine day as it covers a large distance with few sheltering spots along the canal. Although these days it's hardly the most fashionable part of town, this passes through one of the city's first Georgian squares for a flavor of the Northside, living in the shadow of the more affluent Southside. START: **Bus 13, 13A & 19 to Botanic Gardens.**

① kids ★★★ National Botanic Gardens. Going strong for more than 200 years, the gardens cover a mammoth 20 hectares (50 acres) with over 20,000 species of rare and cultivated plants from all over the world. Depending on what's in season, you might see rhododendrons, roses, vast conifers, and Chinese plants. The immense curvilinear wall is amazing: a huge glass house with curved walls comprising over 8,400 panes of glass, renovated in 1995. Imagine cleaning that lot. The palm house opposite is just as stunning (incredible to think that it came as a flat pack from Scotland). The Visitor Center hosts exhibitions and talks. 🕐 *90 min. Botanic Rd, Glasnevin.* ☎ *01-857 0909. www.botanic gardens.ie. Free admission. Feb–Oct daily 9am–6pm; Nov–Jan daily* 9am–4.30pm. Free tours Sun noon & 2.30pm.

②' kids Garden Catering. The Visitor Center's huge café is great for resting weary feet (or drying off). Refuel with hot drinks and snacks, or hot meals such as jacket potatoes between 12–2.30pm; a friendly canteen. *National Botanic Gardens,* ☎ *01-857 0909. $.*

③ ★ Pyramid Church. I first came across this astounding church when exploring the area. It looks, from a distance, like an ebony pyramid in the middle of a roundabout, and that's pretty much what it is. Made from dark timber, Our Lady of Dolores (its official name) was built

There are over 8,400 panes of glass in the curvilinear wall.

in 1972. Although the interior lacks ornate charm, its etched glass windows around the perimeter, depicting the 14 Stations of the Cross (the final hours of Jesus before crucifixion) make an interesting perusal. ⏱ *20 min. Cnr Botanic Ave & Botanic Rd. 9am–6.30pm; Mass Sun 10am & 11.30am, 6.30pm.*

④ ★★★ Glasnevin Cemetery.

Not as morbid as it sounds: a tour (self-guided or with a guide) of the cemetery brings Ireland's history, ironically, to life. This vast burial ground opened its gates in 1832, after the efforts of Daniel O'Connell to allow Catholics the first chance to be buried in their own cemetery. Before that, the wealthy were buried in Protestant graveyards; the poor by the roadside. Covering 52 hectares (128 acres), an estimated 1.5 million people lie here, half of those in unmarked graves. Luminaries from Ireland's history interred

Ornate Celtic crosses at Glasnevin Cemetery.

here include: O'Connell (see p 25) himself, in an ornate crypt decorated with Celtic art; Michael Collins, whose grave is always covered with fresh flowers; Charles Stuart Parnell (see p 24), marked by a huge stone; former president Eamon DeValera, whose gravestone is often vandalized; and Bobby Sands and the IRA hunger-strikers of the 1980s. Amongst the non-denominational, rich and poor, cross-party cast of thousands, admire the stonework and ornate crosses while you pick your way through the rows. I'm not usually a fan of guided tours, but this twice-weekly one is unmissable. ⏱ *90 min. Glasnevin Rd.* ☎ *01-830 1133. www.glasnevin-cemetery.ie. Free admission. Daily 8am–6pm; tours Wed & Fri 2.30pm.*

⑤ ★ Gravediggers Pub. One of

my favorite suburban pubs, this has been run by the same family since opening in 1833. Adjacent to the cemetery, the local custom to "pop in" before a funeral meant that corpses, allegedly, were left forgotten on the roadside prompting a law that locals had to be buried before noon. Tasty bar food is served lunchtimes and early evenings. *1 Prospect Square.* ☎ *01-830 7978. $.*

⑥ ★ Royal Canal. Join the Royal

Canal from Prospect Botanic Rd, and enjoy a serene walk along the north bank. The several locks along the way dating back to the 1790s are still hand-operated, with usually a fair smattering of ducks and the occasional swan. Peer over the canal and see the infamous **Mountjoy Prison**, which has hosted many a famous name, including Brendan Behan (see bullet ⑦). The western stretch is currently being restored and will take many more years to complete, including bridges replaced with higher ones so boats can pass under. It will eventually link the River Liffey with the Shannon. It gets more untouched as you head west from this point but, should you fancy the walk, avoid it after dark.

❼ ★★ Brendan Behan sculpture. Of the countless statues, sculptures, and busts of famous faces scattered around Dublin, this is my favorite. Unveiled by Prime Minister Bertie Ahern in 2003 on the 80th anniversary of Behan's birth, it commemorates the author of *Borstal Boy* (among other books) who was notorious not only as a great writer, but also as a revolutionary and a drinker. The former earned him a spell in Mountjoy Prison (caught smuggling explosives to England), the latter an early grave (he died at the age of 41) and many tales of his fondness of the bottle. The life-size sculpture depicts him sitting on a bench talking to a pigeon. For a man who lived life as a hell-raiser, this peaceful setting always makes me smile as I sit down on the bench next to him.

❽ ★ GAA Museum. It's hard to miss the huge Croke Park stadium as you walk east along the Royal Canal. Even if you've already visited and taken the stadium tour (*see p 132*) it's worth noting the amazing history of this sporting venue. Built by volunteers to promote Gaelic games, from initial meetings in 1884, Croke Park has played a major part in Irish nationalist history as it hosted decades of Gaelic football and hurling. Its founding members could well be turning in their graves if they realize that, after much discussion and extra money from the government in recent years, they are now hosting international football (soccer) and rugby matches while the Landsdowne Road

Royal Canal with Croke Park in the background.

stadium undergoes redevelopment *(see p 17)*.

❾ Mountjoy Square. Though now rather shabby and off the beaten track, this area was the epitome of fashionable Dublin until well into the 19th century. Originally known as Gardiner's Square, after the founder Luke Gardiner, building began in 1792 in typical Georgian style: 18 houses on each side of a uniform square. Today, much of it has been converted into flats and decline has set in. The south side of the square is the most changed, although the eastern side retains much of its original charm. Former residents include the great stuccodore Charles Thorpe (nos 12 and 22), who worked on City Hall, and the writer Sean O'Casey, who rented a room in (now demolished) number 35.

Renewed **Docklands**

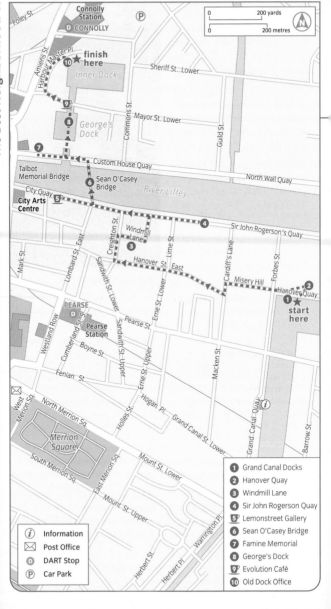

1 Grand Canal Docks
2 Hanover Quay
3 Windmill Lane
4 Sir John Rogerson Quay
5 Lemonstreet Gallery
6 Sean O'Casey Bridge
7 Famine Memorial
8 George's Dock
9 Evolution Café
10 Old Dock Office

(i) Information
✉ Post Office
D DART Stop
P Car Park

Like many other European cities, Dublin is in full swing regenerating its docks, a huge project with cranes crowding the skyline and pile drivers the normal sounds. But this promises to have a great effect on the city, transforming the docks into the Docklands, from a no-go area since the 1970s with only memories of thriving seafaring trade, to a neighborhood with entertainment, pricey studio flats, and wine bars. The old-timers might shudder at the change, but this promises to enhance a forgotten quarter and, as the planners would wish, shift the focal point of the area farther east. START: **Bus 2, 3 & 77 to Ringsend Rd/Grand Canal Dock.**

① ★★ Grand Canal Docks.
Grand Canal Square, now the city's largest paved public square, is a good point to observe the docks and the surfeit of rebuilding in the area. Designed by top US architect Martha Schwartz, this newly established garden opened in 2007 with red paved walkways, giant red rods (I call them the glowing chopsticks), a water feature, and plants. Hint: Come back at night to see the "chopsticks" lit up and the gorgeous reflections on the still water. A new theatre, designed by Daniel Libeskind, is being built to the west side of the square and is due to open in 2008, along with a luxury hotel, upmarket residential blocks, restaurants and stores. **Surfdock**, located in a boat on the south side of the docks and accessed from Pearse St, offers taster sessions for adults in windsurfing within the docks. *Surfdock.* ☎ *01-667 0988. www.surfdock.ie.*

② ★ Hanover Quay.
U2 pilgrimage part I: Yes it's a building site (and promises to be one until at least 2011) but the small unobtrusive studio opposite is the official Dublin studios of the Dublin-born superstars, until their move in 2009 to the flashy U2 Tower close by. Fans (and even fans from 20 years ago like me) will like the graffiti on the opposite wall, trying to mimic their more famous ex-studios on Windmill Lane (see bullet ③). If you

Grand Canal "chopsticks".

hang out long enough, the local construction workers will probably think you're mad, but you might catch a glimpse of Bono and clan.

③ kids ★ Windmill Lane and the U2 wall.
U2 pilgrimage part II: Fans from around the world were encouraged to leave their tributes to the band on the walls of 4 Windmill Lane, their studios throughout the 1980s. Now the entire street is covered, difficult to distinguish

between what relates to U2, and what is simply the work of graffiti artists getting carte blanche to create. It really is a stunning image, although I wonder how much the neighbors appreciate it.

④ kids ★ Sir John Rogerson Quay. The life-size iron sculpture **The Linesman** by Dony Mac-Manus depicts the docker heaving in the ropes, dragging something presumably extremely heavy given the look of effort on his face. The quay, developed in 1713 by former MP Sir John Rogerson, also has the **DDDA offices** (Dublin Docklands Development Agency) from where it's possible to get a map of the area. Work on a huge new sculpture by UK artist Anthony Gormley commenced in 2008. No doubt it will get the usual Dubliners' nickname treatment in due course.

⑤ ★★ The Lemonstreet Gallery. Paintings, prints, and etchings by local and international artists furnish the walls, and the 1st floor café has gourmet sandwiches, wraps, and coffee. All the artwork is for sale, and it's a lovely bright venue with a Liffey view. *24–26 City Quay.* ☎ *01-671 0240. www.lemonstreet.com $.*

⑥ kids ★ Sean O'Casey Bridge. Honoring the great Dublin writer, this is the newest bridge and the third since 2000. As you walk the 100m (110 yards) to cross the Liffey, mutter to yourself, "The whole world is in a terrible state of chassis", from O'Casey's *Juno and the Paycock*. Feel the bridge's slight sway, no doubt prompting the nickname "Quiver on the River" from locals (also relates to the Millennium Bridge). The graceful construction opens into two sections, swinging 90 degrees to allow tall boats to pass through.

⑦ ★★ Famine Memorial. This striking bronze sculpture commemorates the Great Famine of the mid-19th century, when Ireland lost millions of people due to starvation and emigration. It's fitting that it stands here, as these docks were where many desperate people left on US-bound ships seeking work and

The striking Famine Memorial.

Old Dock Office, now comfortable bar and restaurant.

survival. The memorial, created by Rowan Gillespie, was allegedly commissioned for Boston, Massachusetts, but their local mayor found it "too depressing", hence it stayed. Depicting several hunger-ravaged people, plus a dog, the haunting image stands ironically in the shadow of the **International Financial Services Centre (IFSC)**. The symbolism is harsh (intentionally?) given that this is the engine room of the modern Irish economy containing 110 banks, and trading an estimated 900 billion in 2006. Amazing what changes occur in 150 years.

8 ★★ George's Dock. Constructed in 1796, this area adjacent to Customs House dock was filled with warehouses storing rum, wine, whiskey, and sugar. A huge fire in 1833 caused burning spirits to flow into the river, and it was noted that "the Liffey was a sheet of flame for half its breadth" and visible for miles. There must have been a lot of "what a waste" comments flying round that night. In 1987 the government established the Customs

House Docks Development Authority, who later developed the IFSC.

9 kids ★★ Evolution Café. Part of the O'Brien's sandwich chain, and within the IFSC (so lots of city types getting takeaways) this branch has a tiny balcony overlooking George's Dock. Even if you're not hungry, have a coffee, take a seat on the balcony, and enjoy the view. *3 George's Dock, IFSC.* ☎ *01-670 1900. $.*

10 ★ Old Dock Office. The old Dock Offices have been beautifully restored and now house the Harbourmaster Bar and Restaurant (*see p 106*). It's great to see buildings like this: well preserved, respecting its past, and making it into something functional that people can enjoy. Dubliners also seem to like it, even those resenting the great swathes of rebuilding that could take the old character away. Drop in for a drink by the open fire, or return later in the evening for dinner.

Liffey **Boardwalk**

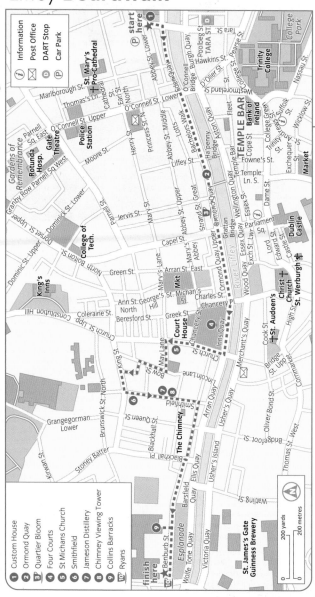

Legend

- ⓘ Information
- ☒ Post Office
- Ⓓ DART Stop
- Ⓟ Car Park

start here ★❶

Walk stops:

1. Custom House
2. Ormond Quay
3. Quartier Bloom
4. Four Courts
5. St Michans Church
6. Smithfield
7. Jameson Distillery
8. Chimney Viewing Tower
9. Collins Barracks
10. Ryans

finish here ★⓾

0 — 200 yards
0 — 200 metres

St. James's Gate
Guinness Brewery

Trinity College

TEMPLE BAR

Dublin Castle

Christ Church

The Chimney

Built as part of a **Millennium project**, the Liffey Boardwalk is a good start for exploring the Liffey's north bank without traffic interference. It makes a frantically busy street seem peaceful, breathes new life into the area and offers a better opportunity to peruse the river itself. Considering recent flooding around the world, it's all the more remarkable that the Liffey has never flooded since the river wall was built in 1800, especially considering the city's high rainfall. This walk starts with an impressive landmark, ending at one of the city's finest museums. START: **Bus 53A to Custom House Quay or 15, 45 & 65 to Eden Quay.**

① ★★ Custom House. You'll be hard pushed to miss this building, dominating as it does the north quay: it's architecturally one of the most important buildings in Dublin. Designed by Englishman James Gandon and completed in 1791, its exterior is richly adorned with sculptures with strong Irish themes. Take a good look at Hibernia seen embracing Britannia while Neptune drives away famine and despair. It was positioned on this part of the quay in an attempt to shift the city's center slightly further east, which angered city merchants at the time. For the best view, gaze at this scene at night from the south side of the river.

Sun setting on the Custom House.

② ★ Ormond Quay. Perhaps the loveliest example of how this area has been developed, just past the Ha'penny Bridge (*see p 19*), is the **Hags with the Bags** sculpture—two ladies resting on a bench complete with Arnotts shopping bags. The lovely new Italian quarter, **Quartier Bloom,** is a little enclave of eateries with outdoors tables nestled around a small alleyway, complete with a huge mural of the Last Supper on the wall outside. This adds a very Mediterranean feel to the place, and locals love to pop in for lunch, a coffee, or to stock up on Italian foodstuffs.

③ kids **★★ Quartier Bloom.** For a coffee break, lunch, or ice cream, find a spot in this Italian Quarter and dine al fresco. On sunny days this place is very popular, so choose your venue, pull up a chair, order a latte, and get feasting. *Assorted venues, Lower Ormond Quay. $–$$.*

④ ★★ Four Courts. A Dublin landmark with its large drum and shallow dome, this building originally held the four divisions that made up the judicial system. Designed by James Gandon (see Customs House), the imposing exterior is enhanced by Edward Smyth's sculptures, with Moses flanked by Justice and Mercy on the main pediment. Destroyed by fire during the Civil War of 1921, the building was restored with few

changes to the outside. The interior, although open to the public (strictly no photos allowed), is a little disappointing.

⑤ kids ★★ St Michans Church. Around the corner, St Michans is the oldest parish church on the Northside, dating back to 1095. Pop in and see the organ that (legend has it) Handel practiced on for his first performance of *The Messiah*. The interior has changed little since Victorian times, and is even more serene with few visitors around. A highlight is the guided tour of the vaults, down steep stone steps, containing mummified bodies and a couple of skulls. With its spooky ambience, it's quite believable that Bram Stoker, author of *Dracula*, got inspiration when visiting the vaults with his family. Some years ago it may well have been possible to shake the hands of the corpse (as my cousin claims) but these days it's "look but don't touch". *Church St.* ☎ *01-872 4154. Free admission. Tours: €3.50 adults, €3 concs, €2.50 children. Mar–Oct: Mon–Fri 10am–12.30pm & 2–4.30pm; Sat 10am–12.30pm. Nov–Feb: Mon–Fri 12.30–3.30pm, Sat 10am–12.30pm.*

⑥ ★ Smithfield. Turn left up Arran Street West to the most recent development of stylish apartments on the Northside, which some locals love and some hate: Smithfield is the original wide cobbled street where horses and cattle have been traded since 1664. These days, the traditional Horse Market (the largest in Europe) still takes place here on the first Sunday of the month, when travelers and villagers from all over Ireland come to trade. The rest of the month it's a peaceful urban retreat with newly built studio flats and tasteful lighting. It also hosts the occasional concert, Christmas market and ice-rink in winter. *Luas: Smithfield.*

⑦ kids ★ The Old Jameson Distillery. Well established on the tourist trail, a visit to the distillery gives a crash course in the making of the "water of life" (whiskey) through an entertaining guided tour. The introductory video gives a potted history since Jameson's was set up in 1780 by John Jameson, a Scot, no less. The tour shows the huge casks, a model of the cat used to catch mice, and a description of distilling methods. If you fancy taking part in the taste test (to distinguish the

Refurbished cobbles at Smithfield.

A painted cart at the Jameson Distillery.

difference between Scotch, American, and Irish whiskeys) then make sure you stick up your hand to volunteer at the beginning. A complimentary drink is served in the bar afterwards although the offer of it served with cranberry juice upsets purists like me. *Bow St, Smithfield.* ☎ *01-807 2355. www.jamesonwhiskey.com. €9.75 adults, €8 concs, €6 children (aged 2–17). Family (2 adults & 4 children) €23. Open 9am–6pm. Regular tours approx 9.30am–5.15pm.*

8 ★★ Chimney Viewing Tower.

Take the lift to the top of the 56m (185 ft) high Jameson's Distillery Chimney for 360° panoramic views. It's a shame that the top two floors are glass-enclosed, but it's one of the few places in Dublin with such an expansive view. The chimney is now operated by the adjacent Park Inn Hotel. The dark exterior looks striking, especially in the midst of redeveloped Smithfield. *Park Inn, Smithfield.* ☎ *01-817 3838. €5 adults, €3.50 concs. Mon–Sat 10am–5.30pm, Sun 11am–5.30pm.*

9 kids ★★★ Collins Barracks.

Hosting the Museum of Decorative Arts and History, this is one of the three National Museums often forgotten about, but well worth a visit. Built on the site of the neo-classical barracks named after Michael Collins, this opened as a museum in 1997.

Highlights include one of the world's largest collections of Irish silver, the Lord Chancellor's Mace, 250 years of Irish clothing and jewelry, costumed soldiers and weaponry, and my personal favorite "**What's In Store.**" Make a special effort to save time for this, a visible storage display cabinet with an astounding 16,000 relics from the National Museums' collection. The cases are divided into eras and nationalities, with a vast range including Indian ceremonial art, Japanese Samurai, and Persian miniatures. Get a drink and snack from the café and take them to the seats in the vast courtyard. On your way out, look out for the oldest letter box in Ireland. *Collins Barracks, Benburb St.* ☎ *01-677 7444. www. museum.ie. Free admission. Tue–Sat 10am–5pm; Sun 2–5pm. Tours: daily 3pm, €2. Luas; Museum.*

10 ★ Ryan's.

Built in 1896 this is one of Dublin's oldest pubs, and still has original Victorian fittings and a mahogany interior. Have a cozy pint, snack, or steak and remember that JFK, Bill Clinton, and George Bush Senior also drank here. *28 Parkgate St.* ☎ *01-677 6097. $–$$.*

Collins Barracks, now home to the National Museum.

Around Grafton Street

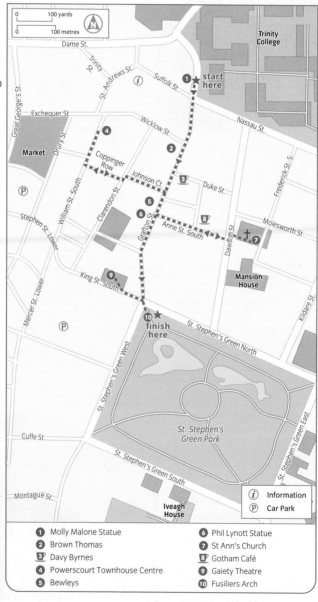

| 0 | 100 yards |
| 0 | 100 metres |

1 Molly Malone Statue
2 Brown Thomas
3 Davy Byrnes
4 Powerscourt Townhouse Centre
5 Bewleys
6 Phil Lynott Statue
7 St Ann's Church
8 Gotham Café
9 Gaiety Theatre
10 Fusiliers Arch

(i) Information
(P) Car Park

Dublin's busiest shopping street has been rocking ever since Bewley's and Switzers began trading in the early 1900s. It's still famous as a pedestrianized street, surprisingly short yet always thronging. Its owners pay some of the most expensive rent in Europe but they can't drown their sorrows nearby as this is one of Dublin's only streets not to contain a bar (thanks to some ancient planning laws). Named after the first Duke of Grafton, an illegitimate son of Charles II, the balance has shifted over the years from independent Irish stores (many mourned the passing of Switzers) to UK chains, which aren't always known for their quality. Squeeze past the shoppers to notice some of the architectural detail on the facades, especially above numbers 71 and 72. START: **Bus 15, 15a, 50 & 77 to College Street.**

① kids ★ **Molly Malone Statue.** At the northern end of Grafton Street, a constant crowd of tourists gather round to get photos taken as they hang out next to Jean Rynhart's statue, with probably an old Irishman playing the penny whistle. This is the clichéd image of Dublin that storytellers and even historians adore. Molly Malone (known lovingly as "the tart with the cart"), allegedly, died of a fever in the 17th century and her ghost is still said to wheel her wheelbarrow "selling Cockles and Mussels alive alive-o" along Grafton Street. But legend has it her daytime work selling Dublin Bay shellfish was not quite as lucrative as her night-time job as a "lady of the night", where she trawled the streets for clients.

Some say that Ms Malone really existed, and tried to prove that she was a god-fearing, church-going girl. Most are content with the fairytale, the song (written by a Scotsman), and the tarty cleavage-revealing statue of the "Dish with the Fish."

② ★ **Alliance Française & Royal College of Physicians.** Pop down Nassau Street to Kildare Street for two notable buildings. Now the Alliance Française (no. 1), this was the Kildare Street Club from the 1850s. Look closely at the external walls, and you can see the O'Shea Brothers' (stonemasons extraordinaire who also worked on Trinity's Museum Building) cheeky carvings of monkeys playing billiards: a social comment on the

Molly with her wares on show.

"monkeys" in the club? A couple of doors down at no. 6 is the Royal College of Physicians, the club's original premises, later rebuilt with ornate Victorian interior. Although closed to the public, its small display of old medical equipment includes Napoleon's toothbrush, donated by his physician Barry O'Meara.

3 ★ Brown Thomas. Haberdashers and drapers Hugh Brown and James Thomas opened the doors to Dublin's *grande dame* of style on Grafton Street in 1859. Since then it has grown in stature, moved across the road, nearly gone bankrupt, and merged with Switzers, another long-established store. It's now firmly on the fashionista trail, housing international designers galore and the only store on the street to have a dapper top-hat wearing concierge. Brown Thomas oozes style, yet there's nothing snooty about its manner.

4 kids Davy Byrnes. If it's not raining, make the most of a rare al fresco venue for morning coffee. Famous for its literary connections, this is where Leopold Bloom, hero of James Joyce's *Ulysses*, had a glass of burgundy and a gorgonzola sandwich. If that doesn't take your fancy, you can simply have breakfast instead. *21 Duke St.* ☎ *01-677 5217. $.*

5 Powerscourt Townhouse Centre. Take another small detour off Grafton Street through the jewelry alleyway **Johnson Court** to Powerscourt, a popular and stylish shopping mall. This is one of Dublin's finest town mansions, built in the 1770s as a townhouse and office for Lord Powerscourt, and made from granite mined from his estate in Co Wicklow. It's fitting that the center today is home to many

contemporary boutiques, the Irish Design Centre, and an antique arcade: Powerscourt himself was a stylish gent, wearing Parisian fashions and being something of a trendsetter. Enter through the majestic mahogany staircase on Drury Street, with Rococo plasterwork adorning the ceiling. *59 South William St,* ☎ *01-671 7000. www.powerscourt centre.com. Mon–Fri 10am–6pm; Thur 10am–8pm; Sat 9am–6pm; Sun noon–6pm.*

6 ★★ Bewley's. The longstanding Grafton Street landmark is famous for its coffee (Ireland's only café to roast coffee on the premises) and for many of us as being a convenient meeting-place inside and out, but the building also has an interesting history. Built originally as a private residence, in 1758 it was a boarding prep school for sons of VIPs (including the future Duke of Wellington and orator Robert Emmet) and it still contains rich mahogany, brass, and chandeliers. The Bewley family were the country's first tea merchants in 1833; they opened Bewley's Oriental Café as a coffee house in 1927 and it's still going strong. Go to the back of the 1st floor restaurant (**CaféBarDeli**) to see six specially commissioned stained-glass windows by Harry Clarke, with Joshua Bewley's will exhibited next to it. The **Café Theatre** upstairs has lunchtime performances and the occasional evening of comedy, drama, or jazz. Or simply go there for its coffee.

Harry Clarke's windows in Bewleys.

78/79 Grafton St. ☎ 01-672 7720.
www.bewleyscafe.com.

⑦ ★★ Phil Lynott statue. Pay
tribute to the Boy back in town! Thin
Lizzy frontman Phil Lynott stands with
his bass off Grafton Street, a bronze
life-size sculpture unveiled in 2005,
20 years after the singer-songwriter
died aged only 36. He lived in Dublin
from childhood, and is known for hits
such as "The Boys are Back in Town",
"Dancin' in the Moonlight", and
(probably my all-time favorite cover)
"Whiskey in the Jar". Talented, good-
looking, and dying young, the Ace
with the Bass will always be a local
hero. *Harry St, outside Bruxelles.*

⑧ St Anne's Church. Peer down
Anne Street off Grafton St for a striking view of the church, with its bright
red doorway and ornate Romanesque façade. Celebrating its 300th
anniversary in 2007, it boasted
regulars such as Bram
Stoker (who married
here), Wolfe Tone, and
Hugh Lane, plus Queen
Anne. Walk around the
interior to gaze at its
stained glass win-
dows; the eccentri-
cally dressed verger
may unlock the bal-
cony doors to let
you upstairs. Look

Pavarotti's handprints outside the Gaiety.

out for the organ, built by Thomas
Telford in 1834, originally water-
powered and renovated in 2005.
Try and get to a lunchtime concert,
held every week or so. *18 Dawson St.*
☎ *01-676 7727. www.stanns
church.ie. Mon–Fri 10am–4pm.*

⑨ kids ★★ Gotham Café. Stop
by for fantastic pizzas with unusual
toppings at this fun café-restaurant,
with a tiny outdoor terrace. The
funky interior has *Rolling Stone*
magazine covers adorning the walls,
and there's great value and service.
8 South Anne St. ☎ *01-679 5266. $.*

*St Anne's Church, hearing prayers for
more than 300 years.*

⑩ Gaiety Theatre. Detour slightly
onto South King Street to the Gaiety
Theatre, Dublin's longest-established
theater in continuous production. It
began in 1871 with a double bill of
She Stoops to Conquer
followed by the bur-
lesque *La Belle Sauvage.*
Built like a traditional
opera house, with
Venetian façade, the
baroque adornments of
the dress-circle bars
were created by Frank
Matcham, a great the-
ater designer of
the time. Many
famous dramatic and musical stars
have trodden its boards over the
decades, including Pavlova, Pavarotti,
Sara Bernhardt, Jack Benny, and
Peter O'Toole. Handprints of many of
these famous folk are on the ground
in front of the entrance. After huge
renovations in 2007, the Gaiety hosts
musical, operas, ballets, and plays,
with Friday and Saturday nights given
over to the club night's **Red Room
Bar**. If you book for a show, get there
early so you can really enjoy the
detailed décor. Check to see if they
are running **theater tours**. *South
King St.* ☎ *01-677 1717. www.gaiety
theatre.ie.*

Grand Canal **to Portobello**

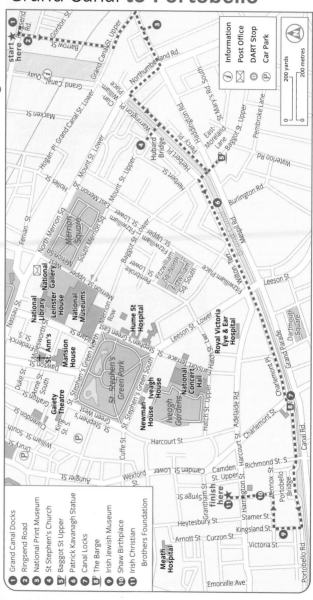

i	Information	
⊠	Post Office	
◉	DART Stop	
Ⓟ	Car Park	

0 — 200 yards
0 — 200 metres

1 Grand Canal Docks
2 Ringsend Road
3 National Print Museum
4 St Stephen's Church
5 Baggot St Upper
6 Patrick Kavanagh Statue
7 Canal Locks
8 The Barge
9 Irish Jewish Museum
10 Shaw Birthplace
11 Irish Christian
   Brothers Foundation

start here 1 2

3

4

5

6

7 8

9

10

11 **finish here**

Twinned with the huge Grand Union Canal in UK, this walk starts in Grand Canal Square, heart of the dockland development, following the canal west with a couple of detours. It helps if you have a fine day to watch the ducks sunning themselves on the banks. It ends in Portobello, an area of tiny red-brick terraces, once a working-class area and home to most of the city's Jewish community—including Leopold Bloom, the fictional Jewish hero in Joyce's *Ulysses*. Today it's known for the huge private Portobello College. START: **Bus 2, 3 & 77 to Ringsend Rd/Grand Canal Dock.**

① ★ Grand Canal Docks.
Explore the paved square, hub of the recreated docklands area. (see *Renewed Docklands p 50)*. Walk to **Ocean Bar**, on the ground floor of Millennium Tower in Charlotte Quay (and pop in for an early lunch if time) and carry on around the back, alongside a residential area. Here lies an amusing and unusual exhibit: a huge concrete model of a letter, written by William Jessop, designer of the docks that opened in 1776, to the Board of the Grand Canal Co. In it, he complains about a wall that was 'shoving out at the foot and spoiling from the backing', which Jessop felt was 'in consequence of the piles not having been driven with a sufficient batter.' His ire is audible, even after all this time.

② ★ Around Ringsend Road.
As you come out onto Ringsend Road, to the right you will see **Tower Craft Centre**, a restored sugar refinery dating back to 1862 and now housing artisans' studios. Opposite is what remains of **Bolands Flour Mills** (unless the bulldozers have already got there), where Eamonn de Valera was in charge of the troops during the 1916 Easter Rising. This was one of several strategic points in the city the rebels used as bases; the mills covered the docks, at which any troops sent to Dublin would disembark. Nearby **Barrow Street** has gorgeous little terraces with very low doorways; peer down **Gordon Street**

towards the old gas station to some of my favorite houses in the city.

③ ★ National Print Museum.
Located in the former Garrison Chapel of Beggars Bush Barracks, built in the 1860s, this museum now houses a fascinating collection of thousands of implements, artifacts and machinery from Ireland's printing industry. Laid out to resemble a 1940s print shop, today's high-tech industry is difficult to imagine when perusing the laborious art of manual typesetting and bookbinding. On the walls are framed newspaper pages from bygone decades, and the staff will no doubt direct you to the 1916 Proclamation of Independence, one of the very few remaining originals, as read out by Pádraic Pearce. The barracks are now a cozy residential

Peaceful Grand Canal docks.

square, but outside notice the railings are made from original cannons to remind you of the compound's former life. On the museum's ground floor is the lovely Gutenburg Café with terrace. *Garrison Chapel, Beggar's Bush, Haddington Rd.* ☎ *01-660 3770. www.nationalprint museum.ie. Adults €3.50, conc €2, family €7. Mon–Fri 9am–5pm; Sat & Sun 2pm–5pm; closed Bank Hol weekends.*

❹ ★ **St Stephen's (Peppercanister) Church.** Walk over the quaint **Huband Bridge**, built in 1791, the canal's most ornate bridge. Take a detour to St Stephen's Church, nicknamed the Peppercanister because of the shape of its dome. An Anglican church, this was the last of a series of Georgian Churches established by the Church of Ireland and built in the suburbs as the population expanded. The church stands on Mount Street Crescent, the name of which is thought to derive from the mound that once stood at the corner of Fitzwilliam and Baggot Street, where gallows were used for executions. Try and make it to one of the church's occasional concerts as the opening hours are, sadly, infrequent. Look out for the lovely sculptures around the square, including on the rooftops and outside the Pepper Canister flats. *Mount St Cresc.* ☎ *01-275 1720. www.pepper canister.ie. Jul & Aug: Mon–Fri 12.30–2pm. Services Sun 11am.*

St Stephen's Church, nicknamed the Peppercanister because of the unusual dome.

❺ **kids Baggot St Upper cafés.** Nip down to Baggot Street and take your pick from one of the cafés on this busy street including **Insomnia**,

O'Brien's and **Bagel Heaven**. Choose a takeaway lunch (and check out the stunning Victorian Baggot St Hospital on the right hand side on your way up) and enjoy a makeshift picnic along the way. A few benches dot the canal, including one with a permanent resident (see below). *Baggot St Upper. $.*

❻ ★★ **Patrick Kavanagh statue.** Located on the north bank, opposite the floating restaurant *La Peniche* (recommended for dinner, *see p 107*) sits a charming life-size sculpture of poet Patrick Kavanagh (1905–67) on a bench, acknowledging his wish, 'Oh commemorate me where there is water'. Like his drinking buddy Brendan Behan, whose similar sculpture (except looking in a better mood) is by the Royal Canal, they are officially remembered in these more tranquil locations rather than their favorite bar McDaid's.

❼ ★★ **Canal locks.** As you walk along the north bank of the canal you may be lucky enough to see a boat coming through the locks, all seven of which are operated manually by lock-keepers. The last commercial barge chugged through here in 1950, but with renovation by the Inland Waterways Association of Ireland there is an increase is canal transport. Once you reach Portobello (also called Le Touche) Bridge, peer south down Rathmines Road to the huge green dome of the Church of Mary Immaculate Refuge of Sinners, and alongside lush willow trees past Portobello College. On the right, the streets become quaint red-brick terraces.

8 ★ **The Barge.** A canalside favourite, weekdays are quieter than raucous DJ nights. Carvery lunch is served every day, or just pick soup and sandwich and take a seat by the water. *42 Charlemont St.* ☎ *01-475 1869. $.*

9 ★★ **Irish Jewish Museum.** Little remains of Dublin's once large Jewish community here in Portobello. But this small museum housed in the old Walworth Road Synagogue has a slightly chaotic collection of artifacts and memorabilia connected to Irish Jewry over the last 150 years, including from Belfast, Cork and Limerick. The first floor includes photographs (including one of my great-great-uncle's butcher shop), old paintings, certificates and ceremonial objects, and Joyce fans should look for the photos of Jewish characters as mentioned in *Ulysses*. The upper floor is the original synagogue with religious objects displayed. The museum's curator and volunteers can help with genealogical research for visitors with Jewish roots in Ireland, requiring all information in writing in advance of your visit. ⏲ *45 min. 3 Walworth Rd.* ☎ *01-490 1857. www.jewishireland. org/museum.html. Admission free; donations welcome. May–Sept Sun, Tues & Thurs 11am–3.30pm; Oct–Apr Sun 10.30am–2.30pm.*

The Jewish Museum.

The kitchen at George Bernard Shaw's birthplace.

10 ★★★ **Shaw Birthplace.** Synge Street is the childhood home of great playwright George Bernard Shaw (1856–1950), author of *Pygmalion*, *Arms and the Man* and *Man and Superman*. My favorite part is not just the decent recreation of a 19th-century family home, but the revelations into Shaw's life and career, including a Nobel Prize in 1925 and an Oscar in 1938. His biting wit, as told via the audio guide, reveals his opinions of his family: his drunken father George, and mother Lucinda who 'could be classed only as a bohemian anarchist with lady-like habits' (and suspected of having an affair with her piano teacher). Take time at the end to inspect everything on the walls, including a photo of Shaw signing the Freedom of the City aged 94, and with Michael Collins in 1922, shortly before he (Collins) died. *33 Synge St,* ☎ *01-475 0854. Adults €4, conc €3, children (age 3–11) €1.5. May–Oct Mon–Sat 10am–5pm, Sun & hols 11am–5pm.*

11 ★ **Irish Christian Brothers Foundation.** Further north up Synge Street is the school whose past pupils include, among others, longstanding broadcasters Gay Byrne and Eamonn Andrews, actor Cyril Cusack, ex-president of Israel Chaim Herzog and George Bernard Shaw himself. *Synge Street.*

Kilmainham **to** Phoenix Park

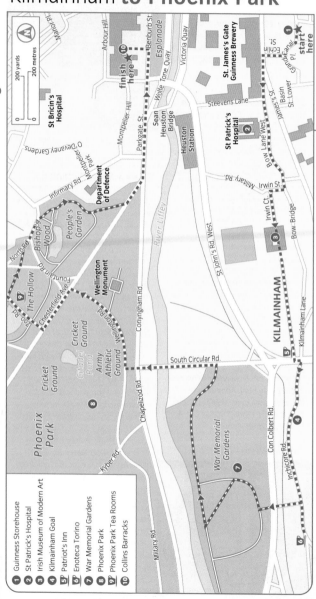

1 Guinness Storehouse
2 St Patrick's Hospital
3 Irish Museum of Modern Art
4 Kilmainham Gaol
5 Patriot's Inn
6 Enoteca Torino
7 War Memorial Gardens
8 Phoenix Park
9 Phoenix Park Tea Rooms
10 Collins Barracks

start here

finish here

St Bricin's Hospital

St James's Gate Guinness Brewery

St Patrick's Hospital

Heuston Station

Sean Heuston Bridge

Department of Defence

People's Garden

Wellington Monument

Cricket Ground

Cricket Ground

Citadel Pond

Army Athletic Ground

Phoenix Park

The Hollow

War Memorial Gardens

Collins Barracks

KILMAINHAM

0   200 yards
0   200 metres

River Liffey

Arbour Hill

Benburb St.
Esplanade
Victoria Quay
Wolfe Tone Quay
Steevens Lane

Manor Pl.

Montpelier Hill
Parkgate St.
Infirmary Rd.
Montpelier Park
O'Devaney Gardens

North Rd.
Bishop's Wood
Fountain Rd.
Chesterfield Ave.
Odd Rd.

Conyngham Rd.
Chapelizod Rd.
Military Rd.
Kyber Rd.
South Circular Rd.

St John's Rd. West
Millary Rd.
Irwin St.
Irwin Ct.
Bow Lane West
Bow Bridge
Bow-Bridge
Kilmainham Lane
Con Colbert Rd.
Inchicore Rd.

James's St.
Basin St. Lower
Grand Canal Pl.
Echlin St.

Prisons, art and parkland—plus a walk through areas of the city you wouldn't normally come across. Starting at 'Guinness land', home of Ireland's most famous export (although now owned by British company Diageo), this walk takes you through Kilmainham, an area under massive construction. This was also an area where the Vikings settled some 2,000 years ago. After a powerful tour around the Gaol, it's a peaceful walk through the War Memorial Gardens which cut through to Phoenix Park. Take on the wonderful exhibition at Collins Barracks if you still have the energy. START: **Bus 51B, 78A and 123 to James's Street.**

❶ ★★ Guinness Storehouse.

Even if you've already taken the lengthy tour inside the Storehouse (see p 15), this historic area is firmly ingrained with the Guinness family. Arthur Guinness grew up at nearby 1 Thomas Street, then established the St James's Gate Brewery in 1759, taking over a small redundant brewery (paying only a little more than the cost of a pint today). He married Olivia Whitmore, a relative of Henry Grattan, in 1761 and they had 21 children—really proving the advertizing slogan 'Guinness is good for you'. Their first family home is close to the brewery. The brewery was later inherited by his great-grandson Arthur, later known as the first Lord Ardilaun, and Edward, the first Earl of Iveagh; his statue stands in the grounds of St Patrick's Cathedral, for which he paid for refurbishment.

A pint of black stuff.

❷ ★ St Patrick's Hospital.

As you come to Bow Lane West, you can peek into the grounds of the hospital, financed by Jonathan Swift and opened in 1757. Then the Dean of St Patrick's Cathedral and governor of the city workhouse, the man better known for penning children's classic *Gulliver's Travels* was at the forefront in treating the mentally ill. This was seen to be the most enlightened institution in the British Isles, for the first time treating them as patients rather than criminals. Still operating as a psychiatric hospital, you can see the façade of his original building, designed by architect George Semple, from the southeast corner, although it doubled in size in 1778 with Thomas Cooley's additions.

The courtyard of the Irish Museum of Modern Art.

Harrowing history in Kilmainham Gaol.

3 kids ★★★ **Irish Museum of Modern Art.** Walk down Irwin Street to Royal Hospital Kilmainham (how many locals refer to it still), now home to a superb collection of modern art. Built on the site of the former priory of the Knights Hospitallers, suppressed by Henry VIII around 1541, the foundation stones were laid in 1680 by the Viceroy, James Butler. This is the world's second oldest military hospital after Les Invalides in Paris, on which this was modeled by designer Sir William Robinson. It was a home for 300 wounded soldiers until 1928 when the remaining residents were transferred to Chelsea's Royal Hospital in London. Opened as a museum in 1991, it has a superb permanent collection of around 1,650 works from Irish and international artists, with regularly changing temporary exhibitions (my last visit was for a superb Lucien Freud collection). Many of the original features have been maintained and it's possible to take a tour to the Baroque Chapel (during summer only), and the Heritage Room, which has a display of the site's history. The vast courtyard is a huge graceful space dotted with sculptures, maybe

including a Miro or two. This is a great area for kids to wander around and peer close-up to the enormous creations. There are also children's activities (complete with crayons and paper) most Sundays and through the summer. **Grass Roots Café**, in the basement, has a salad bar and hot dishes. Exit the grounds through Francis Johnston's West Gateway, formerly a gateway to the Guinness Brewery.

4 kids ★★★ **Kilmainham Gaol & Museum.** Start with the decent exhibition, with plenty to think about regarding capital punishment, then the guided tour around one of Europe's largest unoccupied jails, a harrowing history lesson. This is the site of numerous executions of political prisoners including most leaders of the 1916 Easter Rising, and events occurring here have shaped the country's history. Kilmainham had rejected the old-style jail where many shared a cell, and instead had individual cells for one person where everyone had to be silent, based on London's Pentonville Prison. But it was soon overcrowded, especially during the Famine years from 1845, when prisoners were the destitute caught stealing food. Highlights—and grimmest bits—of the tour are the individual cells that housed so many famous names at the heart of the struggle for independence, including Robert Emmett, Charles Stuart Parnell and Eamonn de Valera. The tour ends fittingly at the exercise yard, where the lives of so many men ended by hanging or the firing squad: these include 1916 Easter Rising leaders James Connolly, Joseph Plunkett (who had married in the prison's chapel ten minutes earlier), Thomas Clarke and Padraig Pearse. Recent years have seen a more pleasant use of the premises, with more than 70 films shot here including *Michael Collins, The Italian Job*, and an opera. Suitable for older children. *Inchicore Rd, Kilmainham. ☎ 01-453 5984. Admission adult €5.30, senior €3.70, child/stud €2.10, family €11.50. Apr–Sep: Daily 9.30am–6pm; Oct–Mar Mon–Sat 9.30am–5pm; Sun 10am–5pm. Last admission 1 hr before close.*

Children's bikes for hire at Phoenix Park.

⑤ ★ Patriot's Inn. If all that history made you feel either guilty or angry (depending on nationality and conscience) then backtrack slightly to a bar which has been the site of a tavern since 1793. Not surprisingly, its name honours the patriots who were incarcerated—or killed—at the nearby jail. These days it's just a traditional pub, usually quiet during midweek afternoons, with a decent selection of pub food. *760 South Circular Rd, Kilmainham ☎ 01-679 9595.$.*

⑥ kids ★★ Enoteca Torino. Perhaps if you need something more substantial, this is some of the best and least expensive Italian food in Dublin. Fresh pasta is made daily, with several dishes every day, plus cheese or charcuterie boards and fresh bread. Informal, authentic, tasty and great value, this is a real local's favorite and packed every night. *9 Grattan Cresc, Inchicore (next to Circular Rd, Kilmainham ☎ 01-453 7791.$.*

⑦ kids ★★ War Memorial Gardens. As you pass Kilmainham Gaol again, cross the busy Con Colbert Road to enter the peaceful gardens, designed by Sir Edwin Lutyens, opened in 1939. The memorial commemorates more than 49,000 Irishmen killed in action during World War I, their names recorded in the granite bookrooms. The gardens are a delight to wander around, with surprisingly few people visiting its fragrant rose garden, fountains and lily ponds. Walk towards the north and when you hit the Liffey, turn right and keep walking where you'll pass the **University Boat House** and then **hurling grounds**, until you exit. (There is a lovely walk if you turn left at the river, although lone visitors may find it too deserted.)

8 kids ★★★ **Phoenix Park.** You may have already explored the huge park—one of the world's largest—with its myriad attractions (see *Best of Outdoors*, p 92). You will enter the park near the huge **Wellington Monument** obelisk, so either cut through and exit via Park Gate, take time to explore and spot deer, or hire a bicycle (see p 29). If you don't have the time or energy, pop into the nearby **People's Garden** with its Victorian layout. *See p 96 for details.*

9 ★ **Phoenix Park Tea Rooms.** A lovely little café, not much more than a simple wooden hut, near the Park Street exit. It has great coffee, paninis and cakes, and tables outside so you really feel out in the open. Or you could take your refreshments and sprawl out on some suitable grassy area. *Opp entrance to Dublin Zoo, Phoenix Park.* ☎ *01-671 4431.$.*

Collins Barracks.

Huge Wellington Monument in Phoenix Park.

10 kids ★★ **Collins Barracks.** Home to the highly recommended National Museum of Decorative Arts and History (see p 57), this imposing structure was originally the Royal Barracks, renamed in 1922 in honour of revolutionary leader Michael Collins. The initial buildings, designed by architect Captain Thomas Burgh and completed in 1706, with additional buildings went on to to house troops for nearly 300 years. Built around a series of open squares—of which the main courtyard is perfect for getting a sense of the scale of it—it once housed up to 5,000 soldiers. Europe's oldest inhabited barracks, it was decommissioned in 1996 after which it was taken over by the fantastic National Museum. Take a break at the museum's **Bramble Café** in the courtyard. *See p 57 for details.* ●

Shopping Best Bets

Best **Bargain-hunting for Fashionistas**
★★ Penneys, *35–39 Lower O'Connell St.* (p 80)

Best **Wooden Children's Toys**
★★ Pinocchio's, *2 St Paul's St.* (p 83)

Best **Streetwear for Well-heeled Teens**
★ BT2, *28–29 Grafton St.* (p 78)

Best for **Haggling over Tomatoes**
★ Moore Street Market, *Moore St.* (p 84)

Best for **Designer Baby Clothes**
★★ Milk & Cookies, *14 Westbury Mall, Clarendon St.* (p 83)

Best for **Handmade Engagement Rings**
★★★ Design Yard, *48–49 Nassau St.* (p 81)

Best for **Full-On Foodies**
★★★ Fallon & Byrne, *11–17 Exchequer St.* (p 81)

Best for **Kitting Out for Winter**
★★ Blarney Woollen Mills, *21–23 Nassau St.* (p 78)

Best for **Vintage Earrings**
★★ Rhinestones, *18 St Andrews St.* (p 86)

Best for **Traditional Irish Penny Whistles**
★★ Charles Byrne Musik Instrumente, *21–22 Lower Stephen St.* (p 84)

Best **Department Store Class**
★★★ Brown Thomas, *88–95 Grafton St.* (p 78)

Best for **Quirky New Art**
★★★ Bad Art Gallery, *79 Francis St.* (p 76)

Best for **Pink Handbags**
★★ Costelloe + Costelloe, *14A Chatham St.* (p 86)

Best **Museum Bookshop**
★★ Noble & Beggarman, *Hugh Lane Gallery, Parnell Sq North* (p 77)

Best for **Trad Irish Music Musing**
★★ Celtic Note, *14–15 Nassau St.* (p 84)

Best for **Gent's Hand-Made Suits**
★★ Louis Copeland, *18–19 Wicklow St.* (p 79)

Best for **Eclectic Market Browsing**
★★ George St Arcade, *South Great George's St.* (p 84)

Best for **Contemporary Irish Art**
★★ Sharkey, *80 Francis St.* (p 76)

Best for **Celtic Jewelry**
★★ College House Jewellers, *44 Nassau St.* (p 86)

Best for **Souvenirs**
★ Tourism Centre, *Suffolk St.* (p 82)

Best for **Gorgeous Chocolates**
★ Butlers Chocolate Café, *51A Grafton St. St.* (p 80)

Best for **Party Shoes**
★ Korkey's, *47 Grafton St.* (p 86)

Glittery Goodies at Chica.

Grafton Street & Nassau Street Shopping

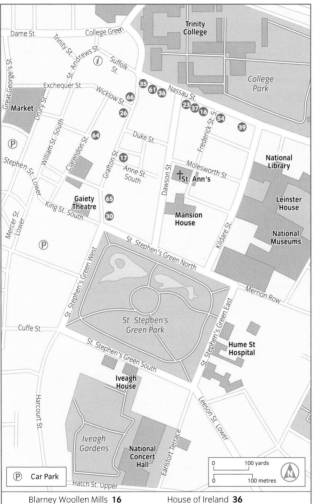

Blarney Woollen Mills **16**
Brown Thomas **26**
BT2 **17**
Butlers Chocolate Café **30**
Celtic Note **54**
College House Jewellers **61**
Design Yard **35**

House of Ireland **36**
House of Names **37**
Johnson's Court **64**
Kevin & Howlin **23**
Kilkenny **39**
Korkey's **65**
Weir & Son **66**

Dublin Shopping

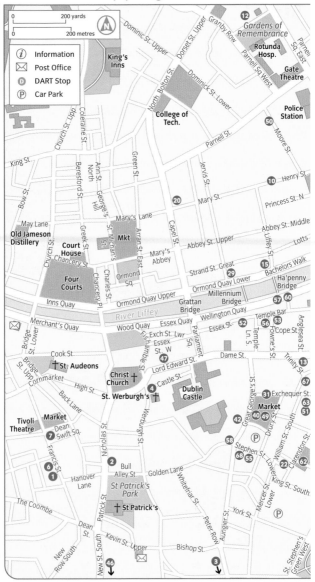

0	200 yards
0	200 metres

- (i) Information
- ✉ Post Office
- Ⓓ DART Stop
- Ⓟ Car Park

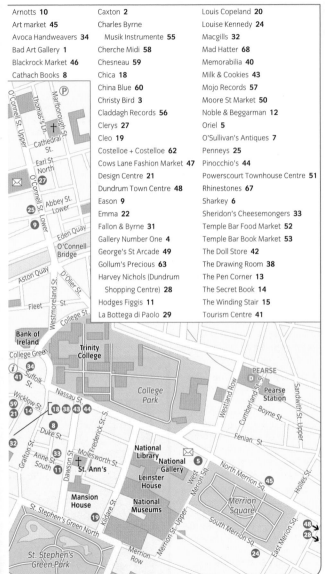

Dublin **Shopping A to Z**

Antiques & Art

★★ **Bad Art Gallery** Vibrant art at affordable prices, this is a bright spacious gallery, perfect for browsing huge-scale artwork. More than 30 of today's best Irish artists have work here, with at least 200 pieces on display. Great fun and friendly staff. *79 Francis St.* ☎ *01-453 7588. www.thebadartgallery dublin.com. Map p 74.*

★ **Caxton** An eye-popping amount of antique prints suitable for serious collectors packed into a tiny space: etchings, prints, engravings, and miniature landscapes dating between 1500 and the 1800s, from all over the world. *63 Patrick St.* ☎ *01-453 0060. No credit cards. Map p 74.*

★ **Christy Bird** Antique furniture has been sold at this family-owned store since 1945. With quirky collectables, you might unearth a Tiffany lamp, old brass phone, or stained-glass fire screen. *32 South Richmond St.* ☎ *01-475 4049. www. christybird.com. MC, V. Map p 74.*

★ **Gallery Number One** This cheerful new gallery opened in 2007 with archived photos of rock stars and regularly changing exhibitions, links pop art and pop music, featuring up-and-coming local artists and photographers. *1 Castle St.* ☎ *01-478 9090. www.gallerynumberone. com. AE, MC, V. Map p 74.*

★ **Oriel** Ireland's oldest independent gallery still sets out to promote and exhibit quality Irish paintings and is renowned for its collection of the late Markey Robinson, a troubled Belfast artist who outsells everyone else. *17 Clare St.* ☎ *01-676 3410. www.theoriel.com. MC, V. Map p 74.*

★★ **O'Sullivan's Antiques** One of several decent antique stores on the street, this specializes in Georgian and early Victorian furniture (with a branch in New York). Chock full of sumptuous chairs, violins, chandeliers, and huge vases, this is for the serious collector. *80 Francis St.* ☎ *01-454 1143. www.osullivanantiques.com. AE, MC, V. Map p 74.*

★★ **Sharkey** Celebrity Irish artist Kevin Sharkey brings a touch of glam to the local art scene with large-scale stunning abstract paintings on show at one of his three galleries (also in London and Ibiza). His high profile brings a high price tag to match. *80 Francis St.* ☎ *01-453 6282. www. kevinsharkey.com. AE, MC, V. Map p 74.*

Books & Stationery

★ **Cathach Books** Member of the antiquarian Booksellers

Cathach Books, for serious bibliophiles.

The relaxing Winding Stair.

Association, this is not the store if you want a bestselling thriller. With second-hand rare books and first editions, and the hushed tone of a library, this is for serious bibliophiles. *10 Duke St.* ☎ *01-671 8676. www. rarebooks.ie. AE, MC, V. Map p 74.*

★ **Eason** Going strong since 1819, Eason's flagship store has a staggering selection over its four floors. Browse fiction, history, photography, and biographies from Ireland and around the world, and then sink into its café to recover. *40 Lower O'Connell St.* ☎ *01-858-3800. www.eason.ie. AE, MC, V. Map p 74.*

★★ **Hodges Figgis** Close to Trinity College, this is a favorite with academics and is, quite simply, huge with a mammoth collection of pretty much everything. Wonderful for browsing, it has a fantastic bargain basement (literally) with cut-price books. *57 Dawson St.* ☎ *01-677 4754 AE, MC, V. Map p 74.*

★★ **Noble & Beggarman** The tiny space of this independent bookstore is packed full of books on Irish art, photography, architecture, design, and art theory; perfect after a visit to the museum and proof that size isn't everything. *Hugh Lane Gallery, Parnell Square North.* ☎ *01-*874 9294. www.nobleandbeggarman books.com. MC, V. Map p 74.*

★ **The Pen Corner** For lovers of fountain pens, this stationery store has been selling stylish writing gear since 1927. It also has a lovely collection of unusual and arty cards and notepaper, and is the antithesis to the computer keyboard. *12 College Green.* ☎ *01-679 3641. AE, MC, V. Map p 74.*

★ **The Secret Book** Tucked away down an alley off Wicklow St, this is crammed with hundreds of new and second-hand books. The owner only buys what he likes, so there's little dross here; great for a holiday read or a heavyweight tome. *15A Wicklow St.* ☎ *01-679 7272. Map p 74.*

★ **The Winding Stair** A famous literary landmark since the 1970s, new management has retained the original style. More second-hand, new books and unusual titles than popular bestsellers, with fantastic leather sofas make browsing a pleasure. *40 Ormond Quay.* ☎ *01-872 6576. MC, V. Map p 74.*

Department Stores
★ **Arnotts** Ireland's oldest department store is now the

National institution Clerys.

largest, after recent development. The Dublin section on the 1st floor has all the local Gaelic games team kits. Safe without being over-savvy, there are decent sections for men's formal wear, household, beauty and fashion, and the La Brea Bakery for those needing respite. *12 Henry St.* ☎ *01-805 0400. AE, MC, V. www. arnotts.ie. Map p 74.*

★★★ **Brown Thomas** The top-hatted doorman at this Grafton Street institution sets the scene, although there's nothing snooty about its friendly service. Great for men's and women's fashions and household gifts. Shop for Ralph Lauren, Marc Jacobs, Karen Millen, and Gucci, before getting your nails done or hands massaged at Jo Malone, and then dining in the elegant Kitchen Café. *88–95 Grafton St.* ☎ *01-605 6666. AE, MC, V. Map p 73.*

★ **Clerys** Located in a listed building on busy O'Connell Street and with bags of history, Clerys enjoyed a huge revamp in 2004 but retains some original architectural touches. Karen Millen, Mexx, Top-shop, East, Principles, Ben Sherman, Levi, and Van Heusen cater for men

and women of all ages. It also has a wonderful homeware department. *18–27 Lower O'Connell St.* ☎ *01-878-6000. www.clerys.com. AE, DC, MC, V. Map p 74.*

★ **Harvey Nichols** With a sump-tuous foodmarket in the basement, the famous London store is the main draw in the new Dundrum mall, south of the center. Very hip, fash-ionable, and label-conscious, the store also has a restaurant that is popular with "ladies who lunch". *Dundrum Town Centre, Sandyford Rd.* ☎ *01-291 0488. AE, DC, MC, V. Luas: Balally. Map p 74.*

Fashion & Clothing
★ **Blarney Woollen Mills**
Top quality cozy sweaters, hats, and shawls in chunky traditional knits and designs for men and women. A good mix of garments includes Merino, lambswool, cashmere, and Shetland wool, plus other Irish crafts. *21–23 Nassau St.* ☎ *01-671 0068. www.blarney.com. AE, MC, V. Map p 73.*

★ **kids BT2** An offshoot of Brown Thomas department store (see above), this has top contempo-rary fashion labels for teen's urban wear, including Miss Sixty, Diesel, G-Star, American Retro, plus unusual styles from Bea Yuk Mui. *28-29 Grafton St.* ☎ *01-605 6666. AE, MC, V. Map p 73.*

★★ **Chica** This is the place to come for beaded tops, dressy fab-rics, and eccentric outfits to make a real statement, or simply to try the chunky bangles or rings the size of dinner plates, keeping on the right side of good taste. *Unit 25, Wrest-bury Mall, Clarendon St.* ☎ *01-671 9836. www.chicaboutiqueonline. com. MC, V. Map p 74.*

★★ **Cleo** A family business since 1936 originally with sweaters from

Traditional tweed trilbies at Kevin & Howlin.

the Aran Islands, Cleo now specializes in natural fabrics and Irish hand-made clothing made by artisans from all over Ireland. Fabulous unique styles include felt coats, capes, sweaters, and bags for men and women. *18 Kildare St.* ☎ *01-676 1421. www.cleo-ltd.com. AE, MC, V. Map p 74.*

★ **Design Centre** The top floor of the Powerscourt Centre has contemporary styles from Irish designers including John Roche,

Cozy woollies at Blarney Woollen Mills.

Philip Treacy, and Pauric Sweeney, plus Kenzo and Jasmine De Milo. Fashionistas will love it. *Powerscourt Centre, South William St.* ☎ *01-679 5718. www.designcentre.ie. AE, MC, V. Map p 74.*

★ **Emma** This gorgeous boutique sells flowing, feminine designs with stylish accessories, where you pretty much know that you'll get a unique outfit. *33 Clarendon St.* ☎ *01-633 9781. MC, V. Map p 74.*

★ **Kevin & Howlin** Get kitted out in top Irish tweeds, specializing in hand-woven Donegal. The store has a fine range of men's wool suits, coats, traditional tweed hats and scarves, plus smart ladies' suits. The store can make to order and ship. *31 Nassau St.* ☎ *01-677 0257. www.kevinandhowlin.com. AE, MC, V. Map p 73.*

★ **Louis Copeland** The Copelands are top tailors who have stitched suits for generations and are famed throughout Ireland. The store carries labels such as Hugo Boss and snazzy Duchamp ties, and also has two outlets in South Dublin. *39–41 Capel St.* ☎ *01-872 1600. www.louiscopeland.com. AE, MC, V. Map p 74.*

Prime Shopping Zones

Centerpiece to the Southside's shopping experience is the pedestrianized **Grafton Street** with Brown Thomas, Bewley's, and a host of reliable fashion chains, all heaving at weekends. Running off that is the alleyway **Johnson's Court** with diamond jewelry aplenty, leading to majestic **Powerscourt Townhouse Centre**, which contains an antique arcade and the Design Centre. Near Trinity College, **Nassau Street** has a good collection for quality crafts and gifts, including Kilkenny and House of Ireland, and **Dawson Street** has bookstores. For antiques, head farther south near St Patrick's Cathedral to **Francis Street**, also with handicrafts and great art galleries. In the southern suburbs, the huge **Dundrum Town Centre** attempts to lure shoppers away from the center, with a vast mall of upmarket high-street names including Harvey Nichols. **Temple Bar** has new outdoor markets, quirky clothes, and record stores. North of the Liffey, the huge **O'Connell Street** houses the department store Clerys, plus Eason bookstore and Penneys for cheap fashions. Near that is **Henry Street**, once a big shopping area but less popular these days, with department store Arnotts, and **Moore Street** running off that.

★★ Louise Kennedy Oozing style, located in a Georgian house, award-winning Kennedy's top fashions sit easily with her own designs in Tipperary Crystal, plus David Linley furniture and Philip Treacy hats. Top

View from Bewleys onto Grafton Street.

class products with price tags to match seduce a select clientele. *56 Merrion Square.* ☎ *01-662 0056. www.louisekennedy.com. AE, MC, V. Map p 74.*

★★ kids Penneys Get ready to rummage: owned by Primark in the UK, this is the place for cheery fashions for adults and kids, at fantastic value. The clothes might not last for years, but at that price, who cares? Hugely popular and always packed, so try to avoid the scrum on a Saturday. *35–39 Lower O'Connell St.* ☎ *01-666 6656. www.primark.co.uk. MC, V. Map p 74.*

Gourmet Food
★ Butlers Chocolate Café Still using the original 1932 recipes from Mrs Bailey-Butler, the small stores around town sell their gorgeous chocs by the box or individually, including orange marzipan, cerise au kirsch, and Irish cream liqueur. Outlets also

Fallon & Byrne for foodies.

sell freshly brewed coffee. *51A Grafton St.* ☎ *01-616 7004. www. butlerschocolates.com. AE, MC, V. Map p 73.*

★★★ Fallon & Byrne   The mother of all food halls, and one where I could happily spend a year, sells everything from designer truffles and fresh fruit tarts to old-fashioned sweets, cheese, charcuterie, and organic vegetables. This has the selection of a supermarket but the class of a boutique. *11–17 Exchequer St.* ☎ *01-472 1010. www.fallon andbyrne.com. MC, V. Map p 74.*

★ La Bottega di Paolo   With fresh produce imported from Italy, this little deli in the corner of Ormond Quay's Italian Quarter has the full range of olives, plump buffalo mozzarella, salami, fresh pasta, and salads. Good for a tasty takeaway lunch, stop by while you're walking the Northside. *5 Blooms Lane, Ormond Quay.* ☎ *01-888 0835. www.labottegadipaolo.com. Map p 74.*

★ Macgills   A cozy little deli with an old-fashioned feel, this store has a large charcuterie counter, plus cheeses, Irish handmade chocolates, jars of herbs, Italian *panforte*, and chutneys. *14 Clarendon St.* ☎ *01-671 3830. MC, V. Map p 74.*

★★★ Sheridan's Cheesemongers   A great place to stock up for a top-class picnic, Sheridan's offers nearly 100 cheeses from around the world, including Irish cheeses such as Wicklow Blue Brie and Knockanore Smoked. The store also sells a few select top-quality items such as Ortiz tuna, Aran smoked salmon, olives, and breads. Try the takeaway sandwiches at lunchtimes. *11 South Anne St.* ☎ *01-679 3143. www. sheridanscheesemongers.com. MC, V. Map p 74.*

Household & Gifts

★★ kids Avoca Handweavers   A feast of decorative homeware, such as flowery tea canisters and embroidered cushions, plus retro chic fashions and a gourmet foodhall. Beautifully laid out, the jewelry, ceramics and Avoca Anthology designer women's wear are hard to resist. Kids clothes and toys are on the upper floors. *11–13 Suffolk St.* ☎ *01-677 4215. www.avoca.ie. MC, V. Map p 74.*

★ Design Yard   This collective of contemporary designers, creating jewelry, sculpture, and applied arts, mainly stocks one-off pieces by Irish designers. The four-floor space includes a gallery showcasing local artists, and there is an amazing collection of handmade diamond engagement rings. *48–49 Nassau St.* ☎ *01-474 1011. AE, MC, V. Map p 73.*

★ **House of Ireland**   Pick your way carefully between the displays of creamy Belleek ceramic vases, John Rocha-designed Waterford crystal, Claddagh rings, and my personal favorite, Mullingar Pewter goblets. *38 Nassau St.* ☎ *01-671 1111. www.houseofireland.com. AE, DC, MC, V. Map p 73.*

★ **House of Names**   The House of Names is a great place to visit for souvenirs for anyone with Irish roots, ranging from keyrings to copper shields. Framed certificates with family name, origin, and meaning take 10 days and can be ordered in advance. *26 Nassau St.* ☎ *01-679 7287. www.houseofnames.ie. AE, MC, V. Map p 73. Also at 8 Fleet St.* ☎ *01-677 7034.*

★★ **Kilkenny**   Drop by Dublin's best emporium for Irish-made gifts and arty finds for home, with a small collection of Waterford crystal, ceramics, and contemporary sculptures. Don't miss the Irish fashions at the back of the 1st floor with lots of crumpled purples and moss greens. There's a decent café upstairs (see p 8). *5–6 Nassau St.* ☎ *01-677 7066. www.kilkennyshop. com. AE, DC, MC, V. Map p 73.*

★ **Memorabilia**   This quirky market stall sells retro posters, famous Guinness ads, Jamesons advertizing plates, and framed photos: Great for stocking up on small gifts. *Unit 7, George St Arcade. No credit cards. Map p 74.*

★ **The Drawing Room**   This unusual little store looks like an antique store until you realize that everything—lamps, mirrors, funky little gifts, and plenty of unusual photo frames—is a reproduction. *29 Westbury Mall.* ☎ *01-677 2083. AE, MC, V. Map p 74.*

★ **Tourism Centre**   Housed in a huge old church, the store in the tourist office is chock-full of inexpensive souvenirs, from t-shirts to posters to Irish biscuits and is a good last-minute store before hopping on the airport bus. *Suffolk St.* ☎ *01-605 7700. www.visitdublin. com. MC, V. Map p 74.*

Kids
★ kids **The Doll Store**   A large range of top-quality miniatures to furnish a doll's house, traditional Teddy

Weekend Art Market at Merrion Square.

Vintage clothes at Blackrock Market.

bears, celeb dolls, and even "create a doll", choosing body, hair, features, and clothes, will make it difficult to drag your kid out of here. *62 South Great George's St.* ☎ *01-478 3403. www.dollstore.ie. MC, V. Map p 74.*

★★ kids Milk & Cookies A new clothes store for young kids, this is designer without being flashy. Expensive but utterly charming styles, the outfits are more like miniatures of good-taste adult clothes in top-quality fabrics and are great if you don't mind spending lots of money on the little ones. *Westbury Mall.* ☎ *01-671 0104. MC, V. Map p 74.*

★★ kids Pinocchio's This gorgeous little toy store specializing in traditional wooden toys, ranging from puppets to a full-on rocking horse and not a high-tech gizmo in sight is guaranteed to bring out the kid in all of us. *Westbury Mall.* ☎ *01-677 2083. MC, V. Map p 74.*

Markets & Malls
★ Art Market Springing up at weekends from around 11am and busiest on Sundays, the outside of Merrion Square is filled with local amateur artists pinning up their

work to the railings. Although not all of it is great quality, you can unearth some gems if you're persistent. *Merrion Square. Map p 74.*

★ Blackrock Market This is frustratingly small, but set to grow. A few dozen clothes, jewelry, food, and gift stalls are split between outdoor and indoor. New management in 2007 has great ambitions to improve the selection. *Map p 74.*

★ Cows Lane Fashion Market Until 2007 this was only a small collection of stalls, but more space is promised in the future. A small collection of young jewelry designers selling funky, punky handmade gear in a wild range of materials. *Cows Lane, Temple Bar. Map p 74.*

★ Dundrum Town Centre This huge mall south of the city center, easily accessible by tram, specializes in popular high-street chains such as Esprit, French Connection, Mexx, and Zara, with jewelers, restaurants, kids' gear, sportswear, and stationery, plus Harvey Nichols (see p 78) as its highlight (for many). *Sandyford Rd.*

Cheese galore at Temple Bar Food Market.

Claddagh Records in the Heart of Temple Bar.

☎ 01-299 1700. www.dundrum.ie. Luas: Balally. Map p 74.

★★ kids George's St Arcade
The former red-brick Victorian meat market is now home to quirky stalls, second-hand records, hats, health food, jewelry, and kooky clothes. *South Great George's St. www. georgesstreetarcade.ie. Map p 74.*

★ Moore Street Market
Hardly the place it once was, Moore Street is one of the few remaining genuine daily street markets with stalls of fruit, veg, and even foreign foodstuffs. Traditional as it gets, stop by to watch the deliveries by horse-and-cart and listen to fruity banter. *Moore St. Map p 74.*

★★Powerscourt Townhouse Centre With graceful history and graceful decor, the center has an antiques arcade, fashion stores, lovely independent jewelry stores, and the Design Centre on the top floor. The Atrium has plenty of eating places on the 1st floor and upper balconies. *59 South William St.* ☎ 01-671 7000. www.powerscourt centre.com. Map p 74.

★ Temple Bar Food Market
Every Saturday sees Meeting House Square in Temple Bar filled with stalls selling organic fruit and veg, cheeses, home-made breads, Irish cakes, and freshly cooked snacks; a relatively new concept, which so far seems to attract more visitors than locals. *Meeting House Square, Temple Bar. Map p 74.*

★ Temple Bar Book Market A small but handy selection of second-hand books in the middle of busy Temple Bar every Saturday, mainly by Irish authors: good for an urgent paperback holiday read. It also has a small number of CDs and vinyl. *Temple Bar Square. Map p 74.*

Music

★ Celtic Note Although it doesn't host lunchtime sessions any more, this longstanding favorite is a good place to get to know Irish music, whether classic, folk, roots, or contemporary. It has a good range of CDs and DVDs, and is an excellent place to find out about live music events and get tickets. *14–15 Nassau St.* ☎ 01-670 4157. AE, MC, V. Map p 73.

★ Charles Byrne Musik Instrumente The charming old gent in charge comes from a music-loving family and hand-makes violins. Although specializing in stringed instruments, this is also the best place in town to choose a banjo, Irish wooden flute, penny whistle, and even a book on how to play it. *21–22 Lower Stephen St.* ☎ 01-478 1773. AE, MC, V. www.charlesbyrne. com. Map p 74.

★ Claddagh Records Popular music store in the heart of Temple Bar, specializing in Irish sounds: a lovely place to browse. *2 Cecilia St, Temple Bar.* ☎ 01-677 0262. www. claddaghrecords.com. Map p 74.

★ Mojo Records New CDs, rare vinyl, old blues, Irish folk, and DVDs:

The Shopping Fine Print

Ireland is a little slow to get moving in the morning, with most stores opening at 10am. Standard shopping hours are Monday to Saturday 10am to 6pm, with no closure for lunch. Sunday shopping, once seen as a taboo in this Catholic land, is proving to be popular with many stores, except for modest family-run ones, opening around 11am to 4 or 5pm. Most stores also open late on Thursday evenings, closing around 8 or 9pm. Sales can happen pretty much year round, with the usual clearance after Christmas, although many fashion stores seem to have a huge "Sale" notice in their windows in the spring and summer. For information on sales tax and related rebates for non E.U. residents, see p 169.

in short, this store stocks a huge selection and is crammed with music memorabilia and posters. *4 Merchants Arch, Temple Bar.* ☎ *01-672 7905. Map p 74.*

Shoes & Accessories
★★ **Cherche Midi** A small but perfectly formed selection of designer shoes, bags, and accessories, from Jil Sander, Armani, Dell'acqua, and Barbara Bui. It's all about huge wedge heels, straw hats, and chunky jewelry, in the best possible taste. *23 Drury St.* ☎ *01-675 3974. MC, V. Map p 74.*

★ **Chesneau** Established by French-born, Kilkenny-based Edmond Chesneau, the bags are top quality, simple styles, and elegant with a good selection in all colors, ranging from petite evening bags to huge carrying devices that accommodate piles of books. *37 Wicklow St.* ☎ *01-672 9199. www.chesneaudesign.com. MC, V. Map p 74.*

★★ **China Blue** A very offbeat selection of shoes and boots for men and women, including designs from Doc Martens, Miss Sixty, Caterpillar, and Ben Sherman. *Merchant's Arch.* ☎ *01-671 8785. AE, DC, MC, V. Map p 74.*

Bags of color at Costelloe & Costelloe.

★★ College House Jewellers

Specializing in Celtic jewelry, this is the place if you want to buy and learn about a Claddagh (Irish love or friendship) ring or pendant. Hugely popular, it gives decent discounts to overseas visitors. *44 Nassau St.* ☎ *01-677 7597. www.collegehouse jewellers.com. AE, MC, V. Map p 73.*

★★ Costelloe + Costelloe

A fantastic range of fun, girly handbags, beads, and bangles in a rainbow hue of colors with an eye-catching, busy window display. Bring your new outfit here and you're guaranteed to find a match. *14A Chatham St.* ☎ *01-671 4209. www.costelloeandcostelloe.com. AE, MC, V. Map p 74.*

★ Gollum's Precious

Designer jewelry from all over the world, especially Paris, with regularly changing displays. High fashion but good quality, using unusual materials such as plated glass, and colourful silver designs. Everything is nickel-free. *1st floor, Powerscourt Centre.* ☎ *01-670 5400. MC, V. Map p 74.*

★ Johnson's Court

Not just one but a cluster of classy jewelers, mainly specializing in diamonds, on this tiny alleyway off Grafton St: try **Appleby** for large-scale diamond creations, **Edwin Stein** for freshwater pearls, and **Paul Sheeran** for watches, or window shop to find what you fancy. *Johnson's Court. Map p 73.*

★ Korkey's

If you're looking for irresistible, fun shoes that would be great for a party, but probably wouldn't have the lasting power to keep going a whole season then Korkey's is the place to head for. These are the kind of shoes your mother wouldn't approve of, but I love them. *47 Grafton St.* ☎ *01-670 7943. MC, V. Map p 73.*

★★★ Mad Hatter

Fantastic hats and headgear from young designer Nessa Cronin, who uses incredible fabrics such as sinamay (banana plant) to make glamorous and slightly wacky creations, suitable for the mother of the bride or a day at the races. *20 Lower Stephen St.* ☎ *01-405 4936. AE, MC, V. Map p 74.*

★ Rhinestones

Antique, vintage, and costume jewelry, the pieces here are unusual and quirky, and all high quality. Pieces include silver, 50s art glass and 20th-century collectibles. *18 St Andrew St.* ☎ *01-679 0759. AE, MC, V. Map p 73.*

★★ Weir & Sons

Longstanding Grafton Street jewelers since 1869, and a class act, Weir and Sons carry all the top names in jewelry, watches, and antique silver such as Fabergé, Rolex, and Cartier. Walk-in shoppers are welcome and service is impeccable. Look out for the original door from 1895. *96–99 Grafton St.* ☎ *01-677 9678. www.weirand sons.ie. AE, DC, MC, V. Map p 73.* ●

Fantastic headwear at Mad Hatter.

St Stephen's Green & Iveagh Gardens

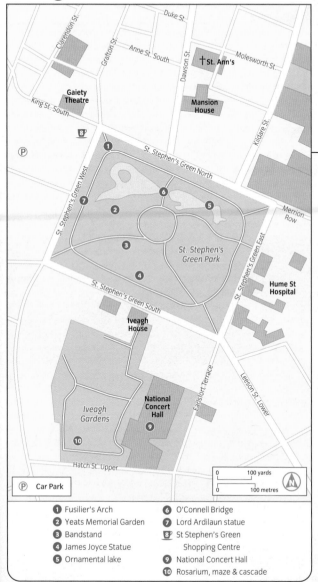

P Car Park

1 Fusilier's Arch
2 Yeats Memorial Garden
3 Bandstand
4 James Joyce Statue
5 Ornamental lake
6 O'Connell Bridge
7 Lord Ardilaun statue
8 St Stephen's Green Shopping Centre
9 National Concert Hall
10 Rosarium, maze & cascade

St **Stephen's Green**, named after a local leper colony, was originally grazing ground for livestock, a venue for the odd public hanging, and then Dublin's first gentrified Georgian square. Built as the locals' private garden, grooms exercised horses and nannies wheeled prams, before Arthur Guinness paid to landscape and open the 9 hectares (22 acres) to the public in 1880. Today's city folk flock to the grassy sculpture-filled open space with ornamental lake, slap-bang in the city center, but the opposite is true of tranquil Iveagh Gardens over the road, exquisite in its near-desolation. Built by Ninian Niven in 1863, this was originally the private gardens of Iveagh House. Few seek out its occasional ornate statues, water cascade, and rose garden, and many locals say it's the city's best-kept secret, although since hosting the 2007 Taste of Ireland Food festival it may not be for long. START: **Bus: All cross-city buses.**

① ★ **Fusilier's Arch.** The northwest entrance to St Stephen's Green is marked by the Royal Fusilier's Arch, a huge Ballyknockan granite arch nearly 10m (33 ft) high. Built in 1907, and a replica of the Arch of Titus in Rome, this is a memorial to the young Irish soldiers who died in the Boer War between 1899 and 1900. Stand underneath and you can read the engraved names of more than 230 who fell in battle. Republicans unofficially renamed it as Traitors' Gate, as this war was seen as a fight between Imperialist and Republican ideals and far from the Irish struggle. If your eyesight is good, you might see the bullet marks on the northeast face around the words "Laings Nek",

thought to be from the 1916 Uprising. *NW corner of St Stephen's Green.*

② ★★ kids **Yeats Memorial Garden.** One of my favorites in St Stephen's Green is the bronze sculpture by British artist Henry Moore of William Butler Yeats. Made in 1967, "Knife Edge" portrays the angular (though tad gloomy) looks of the Dublin-born Nobel Prize-winning author and poet, who was a founder in the Irish Literary Revival of the late 19th century. It stands prominently at the edge of the Yeats Memorial Garden, built as a tiny amphitheater. Look out for the occasional performance during summer.

The names of the fallen soldiers are written under the Fusilier's Arch.

The original O'Connell Bridge.

3 ★ Bandstand. As befitting any garden of the era, this typical piece of Victoriana has cast-iron supports and a wooden roof. Built to celebrate Queen Victoria's jubilee in 1888, it hosts lunchtime concerts throughout summer months, most days. Check the noticeboard at the northwest entrance for listings of concerts; music ranges from jazz to folk to swing. Most concerts start around 1pm, so lie back and enjoy. All that's missing is a decent café nearby.

4 ★★★ kids James Joyce statue. Near the bandstand, poor old James Joyce doesn't look very happy; in fact to me he makes a meek figure, tiny head mounted on a huge plinth. Now considered to be Ireland's most celebrated writer, it seems strange that he was rejected by his own people at the time, who considered him to be far too liberal and out of step with the prevailing middle-class Catholic conservative culture of the time. St Stephen's Green was one of several prominent landmarks that epitomized "dear, dirty Dublin" for him, although

Lord Ardilaun.

he spent most of his life in self-appointed exile. Follow his gaze over the road to Newman House, once the Catholic University where he studied.

5 ★★ kids Ornamental lake. The artificial lake, stretching across the northern end of the green, was built by Guinness as part of his landscaping for public enjoyment. The lake, fed by an artificial waterfall near the bridge, is a big hit with kids, especially if they can encourage the ducks to swim by.

6 ★★ kids O'Connell Bridge. No, not the immense multi-lane highway crossing the Liffey but a little stone humpback bridge over the lake. This was thought to be the original O'Connell Bridge, designed by JF Fuller at the time of the green's redesign, and built over the middle of the lake. It was not until 1882 that the "other" bridge was renamed from Carlisle to O'Connell, after the lawyer who fought for Catholic rights.

7 ★★ kids Lord Ardilaun statue. It's only fitting that the man who financed and created the green as it is should have such an imposing statue. The seated figure of Lord Ardilaun is opposite the Royal College of Surgeons, and he looks in the direction of the Guinness brewery at St James's Gate. Otherwise known as Arthur Guinness, great-grandson of the original Arthur Guinness and born in 1840, he was something of a philanthropist, not least for his purchasing of the green in 1877 and giving it to the capital as a public park. In addition to financing all the work, he also secured the passage of an Act of Parliament that entrusted the maintenance to the Public Words commissioners. It seems that Dubliners have much to be grateful to the brewing dynasty, not just because of the brew.

8 ★ kids **Stephen's Green Shopping Centre.** Of course a picnic is ideal (indeed a must) but failing that, the food court of the glass-atriumed shopping mall has a bundle of food options. For take-away sandwiches try **O'Brien's** and **La Croissanterie**, or burgers and a juice bar with a panoramic view at food court **Foodlife** on the top floor. *St Stephen's Green West. $–$$.*

9 ★★ **National Concert Hall.** My favorite way of traversing from the crowded St. Stephen's Green to serene Iveagh Gardens is via the side of the National Concert Hall (NCH) on Earlsfort Terrace. The hall was originally built for the Dublin International Exhibition in 1865, lasting six months and attracting nearly one million visitors. Redeveloped in 1914 by Rudolph Maximilian in a classical style similar to Custom House, it was taken over by University College Dublin, and has been a concert hall since 1981 although it has only been solely

owned by the NCH since 2006. Its year-round program takes in grand opera (La Traviata), star pianists (Alfred Brendel), and world-class orchestras (Vienna Philharmonic). Despite impressive events, there's nothing particularly snooty about the venue, especially its lunchtime concerts of popular classics. Its decent café is open daily. *Earlsfort Terrace.* ☎ *01-417 0000. www.nch.ie.*

10 ★★★ **Rosarium, maze, & cascade.** Near the Concert Hall is the Victorian rosarium, a peaceful place to sit amongst cerise blooms, and recently rebuilt. A few benches are spaced around, but nothing like the crowds of St. Stephen's Green. This was all part of the private grounds of the Earls of Iveagh, including what was the archery ground used for the International Exhibition. Most of the beauties have been restored over the years since 1955, including the maze, with the sundial as centerpiece. The huge cascade is my favorite, especially if you get there just before noon to hear it being switched on at 12 on the dot. If St Stephen's Green is the public park, Iveagh Gardens is the secret garden, all statues with missing arms, fountains, wooded walks, and Gothic, ivy-clad corners.

Fountain in Iveagh Gardens.

Phoenix Park

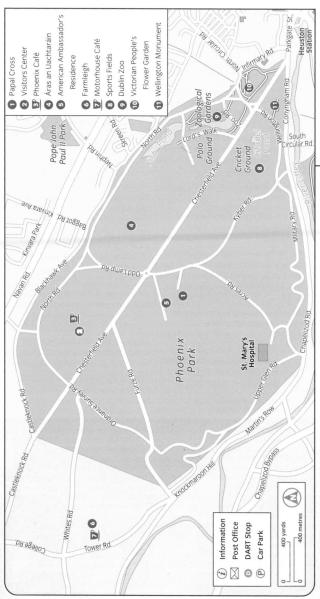

1 Papal Cross
2 Visitors Center
3 Phoenix Café
4 Áras an Uachtaráin
5 American Ambassador's Residence
6 Farmleigh
7 Motorhouse Café
8 Sports Fields
9 Dublin Zoo
10 Victorian People's Flower Garden
11 Wellington Monument

- (i) Information
- ⊠ Post Office
- (D) DART Stop
- (P) Car Park

0 — 400 yards
0 — 400 metres

This park is Dublin's playground, originally built for the rich, now enjoyed by all. Spanning 700 hectares (1,730 acres), twice the size of New York's Central Park, it is the world's largest city park, with tree-lined avenues, forests, ornamental gardens, and deer roaming the grasslands. There's no significance to the mythical bird here: the Brits mispronounced its original name, "Fionn Uisce" (clear water) to the more manageable "Phoenix". There are two separate entrances at opposite ends, but if you enter at Park Gate you can hire a bicycle straight away. At weekends there is definitely more on offer, such as the tours of the President's Residence (Áras an Uachtaráin) on Saturday, and cricket and polo matches on summer weekends. The park is great for kids of all ages. START: **Bus: 25, 51, 68 & 69 (Parkgate St) or 37, 38 & 39 (Ashtown Gate).**

① ★★ kids **Papal Cross.** Just one word springs to mind when you make your way to the white cross: Wow. Its sheer size is awesome, stretching to a mammoth 35m (115 ft) high, weighing 40 tonnes. Startling in its simplicity, this was erected for Pope John Paul II's visit to give Mass on September 29, 1979, to more than 1.25 million people. That's around one third of the country's population, and you can bet that the rest of the nation watched it live on TV. The choir alone contained 5,000 people. Hard to imagine such an event when you walk around its base with few people in sight, but there are photos in the **Visitors' Center** of the Pope's gig in all its glory. Get your eyes well trained: near the cross is the area known as **Fifteen Acres**, home to hundreds of deer (descendents to the original residents from Lord Ormonde's day in the 1660s).

② ★★ kids **Visitors' Center.** Of great interest to kids, this gives a potted history of the park from way back in 3500 BC to the present. There are displays of the grave of a Viking woman and a rock chamber from 3500 BC, both discovered by workers. The park was originally established as a deer park in 1662 by the Duke of Ormonde, who also loved hawking. There are suggestions of

Children's section in the Visitors' Center.

the best place in the park to spot deer. If you've already seen the papal cross, look for the photos upstairs of the Mass given by the Pope, and the chair he sat on. When you've finished here, have a look at the adjacent **Ashtown Castle**, which although sounding grander than it looks, is a compact townhouse dating back to the mid-17th century. Entrance by guided tour only.

3 ★ kids **Phoenix Café.** Although a picnic is preferable in such a green open space, this café in the charming courtyard of the Visitors Center is relaxed and spacious, with decent hot food at the counter; hard to leave once you've found a sunny spot. *Visitor's Center, Phoenix Park, Ashtown Gate.* ☎ 01-677 0090. $.

4 ★★ **Áras an Uachtaráin.** If the Gaelic pronunciation is too much, refer to it as the President's Residence. I still find it amazing that the public are allowed to visit the official home of the President, Mary McAleese, on guided tours every Saturday. She is the first Irish president to allow visitors and this has been the official residence since 1938. Originally built as a summer

Phoenix Park Tea Rooms.

The huge Papal Cross.

palace in 1751, the tour takes you through the State Corridor with busts of all past presidents since Douglas Hyde, and to reception rooms for meeting and greeting and press conferences. The plasterwork on the ceilings is quite stunning, enhanced with two French ormolu chandeliers. All the carpets are handmade in Donegal—the same as ones as fitted in the Vatican and the White House. In the Irish Council of stateroom (formerly the men's smoking room), look up at the stucco ceiling gilded with 28-carat gold leaf, depicting scenes from Aesop's Fables. The Drawing Room, with a glorious Steinway grand piano has padded silk walls and a brass chandelier weighing one third of a ton. Although upstairs is out of bounds, you can't help but feel a trifle intrusive at the last stop on the tour, her private office: The desk dates back to 1938 (with a thoroughly modern computer on top), bookcases groaning with formal books and personal ones where, the last time I visited, she had a "German for Beginners" book and a Slovenian phrase book. Informal photos with her chums the Clintons, a hurley stick, and a Buddha statue add to the personality of the room, so when you leave her home you feel you know the woman. ⏱ *1 hr. Tickets from*

Visitors Centre. Free admission.
Saturdays 10am–3pm.

⑤ American Ambassador's Residence. Built in 1774 this is, unsurprisingly, closed to the public. It's still possible to peek through the huge gates to see the past residence of such luminaries as the Duke of Wellington and Sir Robert Peel.

⑥ kids ★ Farmleigh. Once home to the Guinness family, and then a state-owned VIP B&B in 2001, this 32-hectare (78 acre) opulent estate is now open to the public for free guided tours. Hard to believe that it was originally a small Georgian house, until a succession of well-heeled Guinnesses extended it with a ballroom wing, a third floor, conservatory, and exotic gardens. The tour takes you along hallways festooned with huge portraits, 7.5m (25 ft) high tapestries, ornate plasterwork, and Venetian chandeliers, replicas of those in Westminster. It's funny to think that even such a wealthy family would often live in a couple of rooms in winter to save on steep overheads. A restaurant, café, and picnic tables in the gorgeous grounds give a decent array of dining options to cover all budgets. ⏱ *1 hr. Castleknock, Phoenix Park.* ☎ *01-815 5900.*

www.farmleigh.ie. Free admission. Open Thurs–Sun & Bank Hol Mon. Mar–Dec, 10am–6pm; last admission 4.45pm. Tours approx every hour Thurs & Fri, every 30 min Sat & Sun.

⑦ ★★ kids Motorhouse Café. Once the garage where the Guinnesses kept their fleet of motors, this café now has altogether more modest enjoyment: coffee and paninis to give you a break, with outdoor seating to enjoy the sumptuous grounds. *Farmleigh.* ☎ *01-863 9700. $.*

⑧ ★ kids Sports fields. With more than 2,300 sporting fixtures every year in the park, try and catch a cricket, hurling, or even polo match in the sports fields during summer weekends. The All Ireland Polo Club has its home here, founded in 1873 and is the oldest polo club in Europe. Sit back on a sunny Sunday and watch the "King of Games" in all its thunderous glory, although these days it probably has a lower profile than a tournament in 1909 that attracted 30,000 spectators. The cricket pitch also has a noble history, with the earliest recorded match played here in 1792. Phoenix Cricket Club, founded in 1830, has had its

Get on your bike.

The Best of the Outdoors

Monkey business at Dublin Zoo.

home ground in the park from 1853 till today. Interesting fact: John Stuart Parnell was one of the founder members, and his son Charles Stewart, famous for bringing Irish home rule to the fore (see *Dublin's Heroes p 22*) (was once their captain. The park is a little different today from the days when women were only allowed to watch from their carriages outside. Now anyone can wander through and take in some hurling or Gaelic football, the occasional cycle race or even horseracing. *All Ireland Polo Cub:* ☎ *01-677 6248. www.allirelandpolo club.com. Season: May–Sep, Sat & Sun 3pm (weather permitting). Phoenix Cricket Club:* ☎ *01-677 0121. www.phoenixcricketclub.com.*

⑨ ★ kids Dublin Zoo. You might fancy a peep at some big cats, panthers, elephants, or even mighty giraffes. The zoo, one of Europe's oldest, has been extended recently so the animals have more space. Even the monkeys are guaranteed to prompt squeals of excitement from the little ones. (For details see *Dublin with Kids p 26*).

⑩ ★★ kids Victorian People's Flower Garden. Stretching an area of 9 hectares (22 acres), this is the place for quiet respite and peaceful walks. Laid out around 1840 and opening up in 1864 under

George William Frederick Howard, 7th Earl of Carlisle, this is typical of gardens of the time with top horticultural layout, ornamental lakes, and Victorian bedding schemes.

⑪ ★ kids Wellington Monument. Visible from afar, the tallest obelisk in Europe was completed in 1861 to commemorate victories of Dublin-born Arthur Wellesley, Duke of Wellington. The stone steps lead up to all sides, so rather than admire it from a distance—easy with a height of 62m (205 ft) climb to the base and walk around to admire the bronze plaques on four sides: cast from cannons captured at Waterloo, three plaques have murals representing Wellington's career, the fourth being an inscription. I especially like the "Indian Wars" by Joseph Kirk. Once you've perused the murals, this makes a lovely spot for catching a few rays of sun with views of the lush lawns below. If you think the monument is impressive, imagine what it would have looked like with the statue of Wellesley on horseback on the top, which was planned but shortage of funds curtailed that idea. ●

Wellington Monument is visible for miles.

Dining Best Bets

Best **Journey to India**
★★★ Jaipur $$$ *1 South Great George's St. (p 107)*

Best **In-Store Replenish**
★★ Avoca $$ *11–13 Suffolk St. (p 102)*

Best **Tasty Pasta**
★★★ CaféBarDeli $$ *Bewleys, 78–79 Grafton St. (p 103)*

Best **Coffee with a View**
★★ Bewley's Café $ *78–79 Grafton St. (p 102)*

Best **Pre-Theater Meal**
★★★ Chapter One $$$$ *18–19 Parnell Square (p 103)*

Best **Hearty Soup**
★★★ Gruel, $ *68A Dame St. (p 106)*

Best **Twee Afternoon Tea**
★ Queen of Tarts $$ *4 Cork Hill, Dame St. (p 109)*

Best **Film Buff's Heaven**
★★ IFI Bar & Restaurant $ *6 Eustace St. (p 107)*

Best **Nautical Dining**
★★ La Peniche $$ *Grand Canal by Mespil Rd (p 107)*

Best **Wine List**
★★ L'Ecrivain $$$$$$ *109A Lower Baggot St. (p 107)*; and ★★ French Paradox $$$ *53 Shelbourne Rd (p 105)*

Best **Kids' Fun Fill-Up**
★★ Wagamama $$ *South King St. (p 110)*

Best **Informal Italian**
★★ Enoteca Delle Langhe $$ *Blooms Lane (p 104)*

Best **Breakfast for a Sweet Tooth**
★★ Lemon $ *60 Dawson St. (p 107)*

Best **Dining at a Museum**
★★★ Silk Road Café $ *Chester Beatty Library, Dublin Castle (p 109)*

Best **Hotel Restaurant**
★★ The Saddle Room $$$$$ *Shelbourne Hotel, 27 St Stephen's Green (p 110)*

Best **Lunch for Indecisives**
★ Epicurean Food Hall $ *Abbey St. (p 104)*

Best **Sea View**
★★ Aqua $$$$ *1 West Pier, Howth (p 102)*

Best for **Wannabe Vegetarians**
★★★ Cornucopia $$ *19 Wicklow St. (p 104)*

Best **Eccentric Pizzas**
★★ Gotham Café $$ *8 South Anne St. (p 106)*

A wall full of information at Gruel.

North Dublin Dining

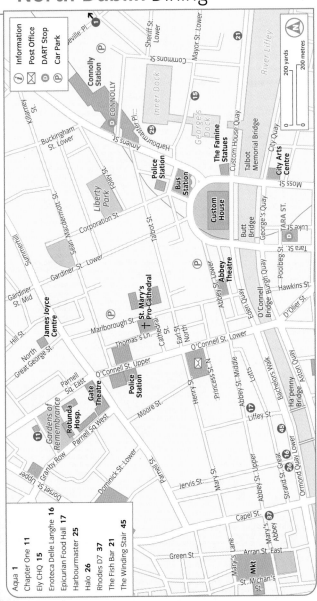

Legend:
- (i) Information
- ⊠ Post Office
- Ⓓ DART Stop
- Ⓟ Car Park

Aqua **1**
Chapter One **11**
Ely CHQ **15**
Enoteca Delle Langhe **16**
Epicurian Food Hall **17**
Harbourmaster **25**
Halo **26**
Rhodes D7 **37**
The Fish Bar **21**
The Winding Stair **45**

South Dublin Dining

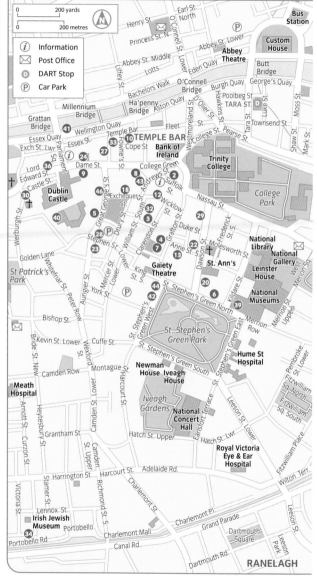

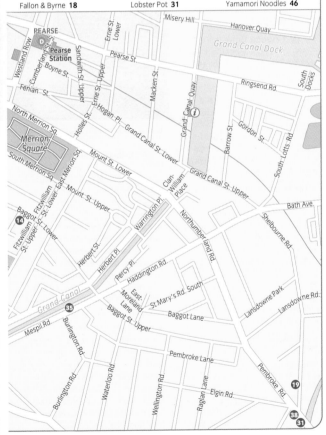

Dublin Dining **A to Z**

★★ **Aqua** *SEAFOOD* In the renovated old building of a sailing club, this waterfront restaurant serves top quality fresh local seafood, such as lobster in garlic butter or steamed whole sea bass, washed down with an impressive wine list. The view is to die for: reserve a table by the window. *1 West Pier, Howth.* ☎ *01-832 069. www.aqua. ie. Entrees €25–€45. AE, MC, V. Lunch Tues-Sun, dinner daily. DART: Howth. Map p 99.*

★★ **kids** **Avoca Café** *IRISH/EURO-PEAN* This hugely popular little spot for breakfast, lunch, or afternoon tea is on the top floor of the stylish homeware store. The hearty nosh is great for shoppers and passers-by with good value fisherman's pie or rhubarb crumble and coffee. *11–13 Suffolk St.* ☎ *01-672 6019. www.avoca.ie. Entrees €8–€19. DC, MC, V. Breakfast & lunch daily; Thurs till 8pm. Map p 100.*

★ **Ba Mizu** *MODERN EUROPEAN* A trendy pit-stop in the Powerscourt Centre, Ba Mizu is lovely for a lunch of soup, salad, or steak, or evening "bar bites" of chicken wings. The stylish venue has cozy nooks and deep leather sofas and is popular in the evenings. *1st floor, Powerscourt Townhouse, 59 South William St.* ☎ *01-674 6712. www.bamizu.com. Entrees €9–€14. MC, V. Lunch & dinner daily. Map p 100.*

★★ **Bewleys Mezzanine Café** *CAFÉ* A Dublin legend and still gorgeous; pastries, coffee, and a full bar is served all day. Spread out with the newspaper in the 2nd floor's dark wood interior, or enjoy the view of Grafton Street from the 3rd floor's tiny terrace. *78–79 Grafton St.* ☎ *01-672 7720. www.bewleys.com. AE, MC, V. Morning–late eve daily. Map p 100.*

Browne's graceful entrance.

★ **kids** **Brasserie Sixty6** *IRISH/ EUROPEAN* Popular for good-value comfort food with a twist or a big hair-of-the-dog brunch such as homemade sausage and mash or famous rotisserie chicken, Sixty6 is lively and informal with an uncluttered decor. I can recommend their Eggs Florentine for breakfast. *66–67 South Great Georges St.* ☎ *01-400 5878. www. brasseriesixty6.com. Entrees €10–€15. AE, DC, MC, V. Breakfast & dinner daily, lunch Mon–Fri, brunch Sat & Sun. Map p 100.*

★ **Browne's** *MODERN IRISH* Sashay elegantly up the steps of the Georgian townhouse hotel to the recently revamped split-level dining room. Browne's offers a contemporary take on traditional dishes, loving its fish (Monkfish tail with smoked bacon and red wine with celeriac fries) and meat but there's also a vegetarian menu: with relaxing, comfortable surroundings, booking is recommended. *22 St Stephen's Green.* ☎ *01-638 3939. www.brownesdublin.com. Entrees €20–€30. AE, DC, MC, V. Lunch Sun–Fri, dinner daily. Map p 100.*

★★★ **kids** **CaféBarDeli** *MEDITER-RANEAN* Try for a table by the gorgeous Harry Clarke windows for fantastic value dining in the cozy heart of Bewleys. The portions are huge, the antipasto misto tempting, salads use imaginative combinations, pizzas have perfectly crisp crust, and even the pasta (of which I'm usually dubious when dining out) is full of flavor. Packed during the day but less so in the evenings. *1st floor, Bewleys, 78–79 Grafton St.* ☎ *01-672 7720. www.cafebardeli.ie. Entrees €12–€15. AE, DC, MC, V. Breakfast, lunch & dinner daily. Map p 100.*

★ **kids** **Café Léon** *CAFÉ* It's easy to pretend you're in Paris in this chic little café, with home-made pastries, and fresh sandwiches on focaccia or baguettes all the way from France. Near the tourist office, it's great for a rest between sightseeing. Pull up a stool by the window and nibble a croissant to suitably theatrical music. *15 Trinity St.* ☎ *01-677 1060. Sandwiches €5–€8. AE, MC, V. Breakfast and lunchtimes daily. Map p 100.*

★ **Chameleon** *INDONESIAN* Sink into purple cushions amid deep red walls for a full-on Far Eastern experience. The Temple Bar cobbles seem far away when digging into the *Rijstafel*, the traditional Indonesian set meal that includes dishes of meat, noodles, vegetables, and seafood in lightly spiced sauces. *1 Lower Fownes St, Temple Bar.* ☎ *01-671 0362. www.chameleonrestaurant.com. Set meals €30–€40. MC, V. Dinner Tues–Sat. Map p 100.*

★★★ **Chapter One** *FRENCH* Descend to the basement of the Dublin Writers Museum for Michelin star haute cuisine, a favorite with well-heeled locals. The seasonal menu has a select choice of Irish meat and fish, and is renowned for cured meats, with divine desserts and a mammoth wine list. Service is unfussy and friendly, with fantastic value pre-theater menu, encased in an elegant hush. Booking essential. *18–19 Parnell Square.* ☎ *01-873 2266. www.chapteronerestaurant.com. Entrees €25–€40; fixed-price lunch/early-bird dinner €35, tasting menu €85. MC, V. Lunch Tues–Fri, dinner Tues–Sat. Map p 99.*

★★ **Chez Max** *FRENCH* A bijou French brasserie in the shadow of Dublin Castle, complete with cheerful chequered tablecloths and tiny courtyard you can share an all-day platter of cheese and hams, or feast on onion soup, mussels, or rabbit stew with wholegrain mustard. The

Eastern comfort at Chameleon.

service is informal and friendly. *1 Palace St.* ☎ *01-633 7215. Entrees €14–€20. AE, MC, V. Breakfast Mon–Fri; lunch & dinner daily. Map p 100.*

★ **Chili Club** *THAI* This tiny restaurant off Grafton Street was Dublin's first Thai and remains popular. As long as you don't mind the next table at your elbow, try the decent Thai curries, spicy soups, and good value early-bird dinner. No booking. *1 Anne's Lane.* ☎ *01-677 3721. Entrees €11–€18. DC, MC, V. Lunch Mon–Fri; dinner daily. Map p 100.*

★★★ **Cornucopia** *VEGETARIAN* Enough to convert any carnivore, this restaurant has been recently extended and is still packed at lunchtimes. Queue at the counter and take your pick from a plethora of fabulous value soups, unusual salads, and daily hot dishes, washed down with fresh juices. Just don't come for a leisurely romantic meal. Closes 7pm Sun. *19 Wicklow St.* ☎ *01-677. www. cornucopia.ie. Entrees €10–€13. DC, MC, V. Breakfast Mon–Sat, lunch & early dinner daily. Map p 100.*

★★ **kids** **Ely CHQ** *MODERN EURO-PEAN* Located in the old Customs and Excise warehouse (check out the renovated basement vaults), this small chain does fabulous wine by the glass with your marinated grilled

whole squid or bouillabaisse. Informal, friendly and very contemporary, it has a large terrace and children's menu. *Customs House Quay.* ☎ *01-672 0010. www.elywinebar.ie. Entrees €15–€30. AE, MC, V. Lunch Mon–Fri; dinner daily; brunch Sat & Sun. Metro: Jaume I. Map p 99.*

★★ **Enoteca Delle Langhe** *ITALIAN* Tucked away in Quartier Bloom (see p 55), the tiny Italian quarter, lunchtimes offer bowls of hearty pasta, replaced with platters of meats and cheeses in evenings; in their words, "food to accompany the wine", and plenty of it. A rustic informal feel, friendly staff and lovely little courtyard complete the mix. *Blooms Lane.* ☎ *01-888 0834. Entrees €8–€12, platters €10. AE, MC, V. Lunch & dinner Mon–Sat. Map p 99.*

★ **kids** **Epicurean Food Hall** *ASSORTED* This packed-out hall has a huge range of options for a cheap fill-up, ringed with small stalls cooking up fresh Mexican, Italian, Turkish, Indian, filled bagels, fish and chips, and more. The central communal tables fill up quickly at lunchtimes. *Entrances: Abbey St & Liffey St. No phone. Entrees €3–€12. No credit cards. Morning till early eve daily. Map p 99.*

Cornucopia's home-made savory scones.

Dine in the Old Customs and Excise vaults at Ely.

★ **Fallon & Byrne** *MODERN FRENCH/IRISH* The top floor of the food emporium (see p 81) has a spacious interior and huge windows. Its menu changes seasonally but always has the 28-day aged Wexford beef, and oysters. Come for an upmarket burger, plush caviar, and white onion and truffle soup with friendly service. *11–17 Exchequer St.* ☎ *01-472 1010. www.fallonand byrne.com. Entrees €15–€30. AE, MC, V. Lunch & dinner daily. Map p 100.*

★★ **Fire** *MODERN EUROPEAN* A huge elaborate restaurant in the old Mansion House, complete with fountain, sculptures, and mosaics, is thankfully backed up by top cuisine such as wood-fired jumbo Tiger prawns and prime aged Irish steak. Professional service and décor help

make it a special event. *The Mansion House, Dawson St.* ☎ *01-676 7200. www.mansionhouse.ie. Entrees €20–€40. AE, MC, V. Lunch Thurs–Sat; dinner Mon–Sat. Map p 100.*

★ **kids** **The Fish Bar** *FISH & CHIPS* Hardly gourmet, but the no-nonsense "chipper" has a few tables outside, which happen to be along the north bank river, and so are fabulous for people-watching. Grab your smoked cod and chips, a glass of house wine, and feast your belly. *North Wall Quay.* ☎ *01-887 8491. Entrees €6–€10. MC, V. Breakfast, lunch & dinner daily. Map p 99.*

★★ **French Paradox** *FRENCH* More like a deli serving food with wine than a restaurant, the Surgery Bar is likely to have well-heeled locals

Earthy Liffey-side dining.

and famous guests from nearby hotels perched up at the bar tasting a fine red with platter of cheese, paté, and meats, plus some hot dishes such as Camembert fondue. Upstairs, the Tasting Room has a more formal layout. A gem. *53 Shelbourne Rd.* ☎ *01-660 4068. www.the frenchparadox.com. Entrees €12–€35; platters €12–€25. AE, MC, V. Lunch & dinner Mon–Sat. Map p 100.*

★★ **kids** **Gotham Café** *PIZZA*
A funky interior with magazine-covered walls and small covered terrace, this is always busy and popular with families. Pizzas here have unusual toppings (hummus or Thai curry) and come in a variety of sizes, always fresh and crisp, plus steaks and salads. *8 South Anne St.* ☎ *01-679 5266. Entrees €10–€18. AE, MC, V. Breakfast, lunch & dinner daily. Map p 100.*

★ **kids** **Govindas** *INDIAN VEGETARIAN* Probably the best karma food in the city, everything in this Hare Krishna café/restaurant is pure vegetarian, and nothing too spicy to blow your ears off. Daily hot dishes include several curries, rice, lentil dhal, and pasta, as cheap as it is tasty. *4 Aungier St.* ☎ *01-475 0309. www.govindas.ie. Entrees €10; takeaway tray 6€. MC, V. Lunch & dinner Mon–Sat. Map p 100.*

★★★ **kids** **Gruel** *SOUPS* Huge tureens of soup and stews with a

hunk of fresh bread make for a tasty meal. Wooden tables, walls covered with gig flyers, and a friendly, slightly shabby air make this a huge draw for students, arty types, shoppers, and those sick of spending big money for a so-so meal. Plenty for vegetarians. *68A Dame St.* ☎ *01-670 7119. Entrees €8–€15. No credit cards. Breakfast, lunch & dinner daily. Map p 100.*

★ **Harbourmaster** *EUROPEAN*
Originally the old harbourmaster's office, the wood-beamed high ceilings, open fire, and cozy old-time feel make it popular with locals. The food is comforting, with steak sandwiches and chicken wings, to more elaborate pan-friend scallops. Stick to the 1st floor of the bar, and grab a seat by the fire (or terrace if it's sunny). *Customs House Dock, IFSC.* ☎ *01-670 1688. www.harbour master.ie. Entrees €12–€25. AE, DC, MC, V. Lunch & dinner daily (closes 7pm Sun). Map p 99.*

★★ **Halo** *MODERN EUROPEAN*
You can't help but notice the astounding sculpture caricature as you enter this hip restaurant, setting the tone; not that it should distract you. Sink into the comfy faux antique chairs and savor elegant dishes such as coriander-crusted monkfish or spiced roast duck. A small venue, but it makes a swish use of space. *Morrison Hotel,*

Dine with a view at the IFI.

Ormond Quay. ☎ 01-887 2400. www.
morrisonhotel.ie. Entrees €25–€32.
AE, DC, MC, V. Breakfast & dinner
daily. Map p 99.

★★ kids IFI Bar & Restaurant
INTERNATIONAL This fantastic
oasis of peace in frantic Temple Bar is
not just for film lovers: The huge bar
restaurant, its walls adorned with
old film posters, has dishes ranging
from burgers and falafel to pasta and
spicy meatballs, all at bargain prices.
Cheap wine by the glass goes well
with everything, as do the home-
made cakes. Go to the upstairs
balcony for the view. 6 Eustace St,
Temple Bar. ☎ 01-679 5744. www.
irishfilm.ie. Entrees €7–€10. MC, V.
Lunch & dinner daily. Map p 100.

★★★ Jaipur INDIAN The best
Indian in Dublin offers authentic
flavors and ingredients, plus superb
service. The original in a small chain,
the menu covers the huge range of
cuisine from India: the best bet is the
Tasting Menu, a medley of starters,
mains, and desserts, from Goan
seafood curry to slow-cooked chicken
in yogurt and cashew, with good
vegetarian alternatives. Ask for a
1st-floor table by the window. 1 South
Great George's St. ☎ 01-677 0999.
www.jaipur.ie. Entrees €15–€25. AE,
MC, V. Dinner daily. Map p 100.

★★ La Peniche MODERN EURO-
PEAN Dine aboard Dublin's only
floating restaurant, complete with
plush red seating, brass lamps,
tiny tables, and lovely service. The
French bistro has a simple menu
including Galway Bay oysters and
duck rillette, and charcuterie plate
perfect for late lunch. Try and book
for the cruises, every Tues, Weds, and
Thurs evening. Grand Canal by Mespil
Rd. ☎ 087-790 0077. www.lapeniche.
ie. Entrees €15–€19. MC, V. Lunch &
dinner daily. Map p 100.

★★ L'Ecrivain FRENCH/MODERN
IRISH French haute cuisine and

The Lobster Pot.

Michelin-starred to boot, this is a
real treat. Typical dishes might be
foie gras with cardamom and fig
chutney, or West Coast lobster
with basil puree, all with an exceptional wine list; the lunch menu is
more affordable. A pianist playing
nightly adds even more of a decadent air. Advance booking essential.
109A Lower Baggot St. ☎ 01-661
1919. www.lecrivain.com. Entrees
€40–€55; tasting menu €120. Set
lunch €35. AE, MC, V. Lunch Mon–Fri;
dinner Mon–Sat. Map p 100.

★★ kids Lemon PANCAKES
The kids are bound to drag you
to this one with its bright orange
interior and fresh crêpes with a
dazzling array of fillings. Go sensible
and have a savory filling for breakfast (mushrooms and eggs) or dive
into chocolate and banana. Waffles
come with fruit, ice cream and most
things naughty, and there's good
coffee as well. 60 Dawson St. ☎ 01-
672 8898. www.lemonco.com. Crepes
€4–€10. No credit cards. Breakfast–
early eve daily. Map p 100.

★ kids Leo Burdocks FISH &
CHIPS Dublin's oldest "chipper"
takeaway dishes up all things fishy
with fries, plus extra delights like
mushy peas. Fish is guaranteed to
be fresh off the boat, and service is

Best view of Powerscourt from Mimo Café.

fast and friendly. A meal of smoked cod with a pickled onion must be one of the finest pleasures in life. *2 Werburgh St.* ☎ *01-454 0306. Entrees €4–€7. No credit cards. Noon–midnight daily. Map p 100.*

★★ Lobster Pot *SEAFOOD* It takes a brave restaurant to bring a tray of neatly presented raw fish to each diner before ordering, but the head waiter does just that, explaining the menu and also accepting personal requests. Renowned for its fresh catch from Wrights of Howth, dishes include dressed crab, sole goujons, lobster thermidor, and grilled turbot, all served in a cozy 2nd-floor dining room. *9 Ballsbridge*

Terrace. ☎ *01-668 0025. www.the lobsterpot.ie. Entrees €22–€40. AE, DC, MC, V. Lunch Mon–Fri; dinner Mon–Sat. Map p 100.*

kids Mimo Café *EUROPEAN* Even if you don't come for the food, come for the venue: located on the 1st floor of the vast Powerscourt Townhouse atrium. Dine on pasta, seafood, or sandwiches on comfy sofas or bar stools, surrounded by three floors of boutique shops and funky sculptures. *1st floor, Powerscourt Townhouse, 59 South William St.* ☎ *01-679 4160. Entrees €12–€14. AE, MC, V. Breakfast Mon–Sat; lunch daily till 5pm. Map p 100.*

★ Monty's of Kathmandu *NEPALESE* Dublin's only Nepalese is over a decade old, with local regulars plus hen and stag weekenders. Delicately spiced with a variety of tastes the menu is meat-heavy, but its monkfish Tareko (barbecued with spices) is famous. Try the tasting menu, or give them 24-hours' notice for the wonderful *momos* (dumplings). Request a 1st-floor table. *28 Eustace St, Temple Bar.* ☎ *01- 670 4911. www.montys.ie. Entrees €14–€21; tasting menu from €45. AE, MC, V. Lunch Mon–Sat; dinner daily. Map p 100.*

★ Nonna Valentina *ITALIAN* Try and get a table overlooking the Grand Canal to watch the swans

Charming interior of Nonna Valentina.

Cakes galore at Queen of Tarts.

a-swanning by as you eat wonderfully authentic Italian dishes of antipasto, simply cooked fresh sea trout, or roast Guinea fowl; a romantic, attractive venue with crisp white tablecloths, simple décor, chandeliers, and friendly service. *1–2 Portobello Rd.* ☎ *01-454 9866. www.dunneand crescenzi.com. Entrees €20–€26. AE, MC, V. Lunch & dinner daily. Map p 100.*

★★ **kids** **Queen of Tarts** *CAFÉ* It's possible to make an exceedingly tasty meal out of pastries and cakes, soup, and sandwiches, in this cute tea house, its counter groaning with freshly made goodies. Inch your way to one of the few tables (it's usually packed) and give in to temptation. *4 Cork Hill, Dame St.* ☎ *01-670 7499. Items €2–€5. No credit cards. Morning to early eve daily. Map p 100.*

★ **Rhodes D7** *MODERN EUROPEAN* Part of TV chef Gary Rhodes' franchise, this huge brasserie has three separate dining areas, adorned with funky art. The menu includes braised lamb shank and crispy whitebait, and a good value set lunch that's popular with local lawyers and shoppers. *The Capel Building, Mary's Abbey.*

☎ *01-804 4444. www.rhodesd7.com. Entrees €15–€25. 2-course set lunch €18. AE, DC, MC, V. Lunch daily; dinner Tues–Sat. Map p 99.*

★ **Roly's Bistro** *MODERN IRISH* A busy, bright dining room in the southern suburbs, packed at lunchtimes, Roly's has been a local favorite for years with top fresh ingredients and a great selection of seafood; try Roly's fish pie. The set lunch is very reasonable. Booking recommended. *7 Ballsbridge Terrace.* ☎ *01-668 2611. www.rolysbistro.ie. Entrees €20–€35. Set lunch €22. AE, DC, MC, V. Lunch & dinner daily. Map p 100.*

★★★ **Silk Road Café** *MEDITER-RANEAN/MIDDLE EAST* Inside the gorgeous Chester Beatty Library (see p 14), this informal spacious café enjoys the creations of Middle Eastern chefs, at remarkably good value. Peruse the display counter, and then choose from moussaka, Turkish chicken, and fresh salads. *Dublin Castle.* ☎ *01-407 0770. www.silkroad cafe.ie. Entrees €5–€10. DC, MC, V. Late morning–late afternoon Tues–Sun. Map p 100.*

Tasteful décor at Rhodes D7.

★★ **The Saddle Room** EUROPEAN The flagship restaurant in the revamped and reopened Shelbourne Hotel (see p 145) has the elegance (and price tag) to attract Dublin's finest. The glam dining area's décor ranges from marble seafood bar to gold lamé banquettes and cozy booths, with a menu using fresh ingredients that's far from complex: try the seafood chowder or grilled t-bone steak, all with impeccable service. *27 St Stephen's Green.* ☎ *01-663 4500. www.marriott.co.uk. Entrees €26–€42. AE, DC, MC, V Lunch & dinner daily. Map p 100.*

★★ **The Tea Room** MODERN EUROPEAN In U2's trendy boutique hotel, the dramatic dining room has high ceilings, huge windows, and a balcony, and the cuisine is equally as uncluttered. Irish produce with a heavy continental twist creates pan-fried quail satay, rock Galway oysters with Guinness ice cream and roasted squab pigeon, and a great value set lunch. *Clarence Hotel, 6–8 Wellington Quay.* ☎ *01-407 0800. www.the clarence.ie. Entrees €28–€40. 2-course set lunch €26. AE, DC, MC, V. Lunch & dinner daily. Map p 100.*

★ **Thorntons** IRISH GASTRO The new-look Thornton's Canapé bar offers a taster of its progressive cuisine; drinks and small bites for a few euros. The main dining area has soothing, chocolate-color décor, setting the scene for braised suckling pig, sautéed foie gras, and magret of duck with mushroom mousse. Serious gastronomes can sample Kevin's Tasting Menu of between 5 and 14 courses. *Fitzwilliam Hotel, 128 St Stephen's Green.* ☎ *01-478 7008. www.thorntonsrestaurant.com. Entrees €35–€60. Tasting menus €85–€180. AE, DC, MC, V. Lunch Thurs–Sat; dinner Tues–Sat. Map p 100.*

★ **Trocadero** EUROPEAN Famous for its old-world theatrical glam, the walls are festooned with signed old photos of movie and music stars, and there's a curved mirrored corridor, plus deep red walls and seats. Try deep-fried camembert and lamb, and enjoy the party—George Michael did during his 2007 tour. *4 St Andrew's St.* ☎ *01-677 5545. www.trocadero.ie. Entrees €18–€30. AE, DC, MC, V. Dinner Mon–Sat. Map p 100.*

★ **kids** **Wagamama** JAPANESE Fast food meets healthy eating; queue up to share long communal tables, and dive into fresh noodle soups and stir fries with Asian flavors. Noisy, popular, and great for kids, the all-day food comes quickly and so is perfect for a good-value hearty fill. *South King St.* ☎ *01-478 2152. www.wagamama.ie. Entrees €10–€16. AE, MC, V. Lunch & dinner daily. Map p 100.*

★★ **The Winding Stair** MODERN IRISH A revamped restaurant above the famous bookshop (see p 77), the huge picture windows overlooking the Liffey make this busy little dining room fresh and bright. Food is simple, such as potted Kerry crab and soda bread, and pan-fried plaice with caper butter, and its unfussy décor (dark wooden floorboards and bookshelves) and informal vibe have made it a popular lunch spot. *40 Ormond Quay.* ☎ *01-872 7320. www.winding-stair.com. Entrees €18–€24. MC, V. Lunch & dinner daily. Map p 99.*

★ **kids** **Yamamori Noodles** JAPANESE Huge, noisy, and great fun, this is a good place to sample fresh sushi, sashimi, noodles, and teppanyaki at reasonable prices. Take advice from friendly staff if you're unsure how to navigate the huge menu. *71–72 South Great Georges St.* ☎ *01-475 5001. www.yamamori noodles.ie. Entrees €15–€25. AE, MC, V. Lunch and dinner daily. Map p 100.* ●

Nightlife Best Bets

Best Ornate Sculptures
★★ Café en Seine, *39 Dawson St.* (p 115)

Best Outdoor Heated Terrace
★★ O'Donoghue's, *15 Merrion Row* (p 118)

Best for Relaxing Cocktails
★★ Mint Bar, *Westin Hotel, West-moreland St.* (p 118)

Best Cozy Suburban Local
★★★ Gravediggers, *1 Prospect Square, Glasnevin* (p 116)

Best Wine Bar
★★★ Wine Cellar, *11–17 Exchequer St.* (p 119)

Best Old World Comfort
★ The Library Bar, *Central Hotel, Exchequor St.* (p 117)

Best Friday Night Boogie
★★ Anseo's, *8 Camden St. Lower* (p 119)

Best No-Nonsense Guinness
★★ Mulligans, *Poolbeg St.* (p 118)

Best Jazz Without Poseurs
★★ Bleu Note, *61–62 Capel St.* (p 130)

Best Bar for Rock Fans
★★ Bruxelles, *7–8 Harry St.* (p 121)

Best Trad Music Sessions
★★★ Cobblestone, *77 North King St.* (p 122)

Best Karaoke
★★ The Village, *26 Wexford St.* (p 131)

Best Venue for Young Local Bands
★★ Whelans, *25 Wexford St.* (p 132)

Best Brendan Behan Haunt
★★ McDaid's, *3 Harry St.* (p 117)

Best Artwork
★★★ Grogans, *15 South Wiliam St.* (p 116)

Best Camp Sunday Night
★★ The George, *87 South Great Georges St.* (p 121)

Best Non-Guinness Stout
★★ Porterhouse Central, *16–18 Parliament St.* (p 122)

Best Gastro Pub
★★★ The Schoolhouse, *2–8 Northumberland Rd* (p 118)

Best Snug
★★ Kehoe's, *9 South St Anne St.* (p 117)

Best Victoriana
★★ Ryan's, *28 Parkgate St.* (p 118)

Most Friendly Central Bar
★★★ International Bar, *23 Wicklow St.* (p 116)

Best Club for Garage and House Music
★★ POD, *Old Harcourt St. Train Station* (p 120)

Best for Late-Night Movies
★ Gaiety Theatre Late Night Club, *South King St.* (p 120)

Temple Bar color.

Dublin Nightlife

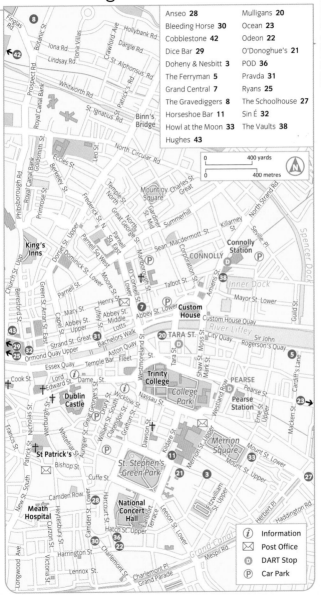

Anseo **28**	Mulligans **20**
Bleeding Horse **30**	Ocean **23**
Cobblestone **42**	Odeon **22**
Dice Bar **29**	O'Donoghue's **21**
Doheny & Nesbitt **3**	POD **36**
The Ferryman **5**	Pravda **31**
Grand Central **7**	Ryans **25**
The Gravediggers **8**	The Schoolhouse **27**
Horseshoe Bar **11**	Sin É **32**
Howl at the Moon **33**	The Vaults **38**
Hughes **43**	

| 0 | 400 yards |
| 0 | 400 metres |

(i) Information
✉ Post Office
Ⓓ DART Stop
Ⓟ Car Park

Central Dublin Nightlife

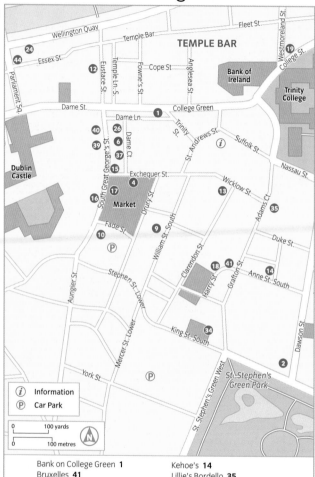

Dublin Nightlife A to Z

Bars & Pubs

★ Bank on College Green

You'll be hard pushed to tear your eyes away from the stunning atrium in this ex-Victorian bank, where the mosaic floor, carved stonework, and cornicing have all been restored. It's on the sightseeing route, so pop in for a pint with above-average bar food. *20–22 College Green.* ☎ *01-677 0677. www.bankoncollegegreen. com. Map p 114.*

★★ Café en Seine
If you like Parisian decadence, Art Nouveau balconies, erotic sculptures, murals, and marble, you'll love this staggeringly huge venue; its many little corners, seats, and niches make it seem cozy. DJ nights (packed!) and live jazz bring in an eclectic crowd; late bar most nights. *39 Dawson St.* ☎ *01-677 4567. www.capitalbars. com. DJ Thurs–Sat; live jazz Sun afternoons & Mon nights. Map p 114.*

★ Doheny & Nesbitt's
Spread over three levels, this is one of Dublin's cherished institutions, a protected building with its fair share of local celebs (with no fuss), politicians from nearby Leinster House, and ordinary folk. With rugby memorabilia and Victorian dark-wood interior, the bar staff happily chat away to regulars and newcomers. There's also a small but tasty selection of Irish food. *4–5 Lower Baggot St.* ☎ *01-676 2945. Map p 113.*

★ The Ferryman
One of Dublin's originals, a Georgian building in a dockland area undergoing a transformation, this was an old favorite of past dockworkers. Now, it's a friendly local with walls of memorabilia, old wooden advertizing boards, sport on plasma TV, a hearty carvery, and a decent little hotel upstairs. *35 Sir John Rogerson Quay.* ☎ *01-671 7053. www.ferryman-hotel.com. Map p 113.*

★★ The Globe
With wooden floorboards and large wood tables, this spacious bar is laid-back and filled with young locals enjoying pints, coffees, free WiFi, tapas, newspapers, and Sunday afternoon live jazz. A DJ plays most evenings, and it merges with club RiRa (see p 120). *11 South Great Georges St.* ☎ *01-671 1220. www.globe.ie. Map p 114.*

Relaxing wine cellar with plenty of choice.

★ **Grand Central** This huge old banking hall has kept the gorgeous interior, with an ornate vaulted ceiling reminding me of a miniature City Hall. It attracts a fair mix of office workers, tourists, and locals, perched on bar stools at small tables. *10–11 O'Connell St.* ☎ *01-872 8658. Map p 113.*

★★★ **Gravediggers** Officially named Kavanagh's, after the family running it since 1833, this bar is adjacent to Glasnevin Cemetery (hence the nickname). Take the left-hand door for the original section, with dark wood snugs, original flooring, and as far removed from a refurb as you're likely to see. It's still charming, with lovely Guinness-quaffing locals, friendly owner, and wonderful bar food. *1 Prospect Square, Glasnevin.* ☎ *01-830 7978. Map p 113.*

★★★ **Grogans** A Dublin favorite where little has changed in 50 years, you'll probably still find yourself among left-leaning journalists, writers, and creative types. Gaze around at the art-covered walls, mainly by local artists, with only the quiet buzz of conversation as a soundtrack. You can order what food you like (as long as it's a toasted cheese sandwich).

Grand Central makes fine use of an old bank.

Local art adorning Grogans.

15 South Wiliam St. ☎ *01-677 9320. Map p 114.*

★★ **Hogans** This laid-back bar attracts a young bohemian crowd, not that anyone should feel out of place in this spacious and unpretentious place, with huge sofas in the windows and DJs in the basement at weekends. *35 South Great George's St.* ☎ *01-677 5904. Map p 114.*

★ **Horseshoe Bar** Designed by Sam Stephenson, the gem in the Shelbourne Hotel's crown has long been attracting visiting celebs, local politicians, well-heeled businessfolk, and anyone wanting a taste of decadence. No windows to gaze out from, just sip a large whiskey atop a leather stool. *Shelbourne Hotel, 27 St Stephen's Green.* ☎ *01-663 4500. www.marriott.co.uk. Map p 113.*

★★ **IFI Bar & Restaurant** Escape the Temple Bar crowds (even at weekends) inside the Irish film Institute. It's a relaxed, unfussy, spacious place over two floors, ideal for a pre- or post-movie bottle of cheap house wine, pint with arty types, or an afternoon coffee. *6 Eustace St, Temple Bar.* ☎ *01-679 5744. Map p 114.*

★★★ **International Bar** A friendly city center bar that feels more like your regular local. The

BORDERS.

BORDERS
BOOKS AND MUSIC
1212 S. WASHINGTON ST.
N. ATTELBORO, MA 02760
508-699-7766

STORE: 0202   REG: 02/65 TRAN#: 3948
SALE   07/28/2009 EMP: 00053

FROMMERS DUBLIN DAY BY DAY
        9349193   QP T   12.99

            Subtotal   12.99
            MASSACHUSETTS 5%   .65
  1 Item   Total   13.64
            MASTERCARD   13.64
ACCT # /S XXXXXXXXXXXX3278
              AUTH: 529515
NAME: REGAN   /KERRIN M

        07/28/2009 03:38PM

        Shop online
        24 hours a day
        at Borders.com

BORDERS.

Returns

Returns of merchandise purchased from a Borders, Borders Express or Waldenbooks retail store will be permitted only if presented in saleable condition accompanied by the original sales receipt or Borders gift receipt within the time periods specified below. Returns accompanied by the original sales receipt must be made within 30 days of purchase and the purchase price will be refunded in the same form as the original purchase. Returns accompanied by the original Borders gift receipt must be made within 60 days of purchase and the purchase price will be refunded in the form of a return gift card.

Exchanges of opened audio books, music, videos, video games, software and electronics will be permitted subject to the same time periods and receipt requirements as above and can be made for the same item only.

Periodicals, newspapers, comic books, food and drink, digital downloads, gift cards, return gift cards, items marked "non-returnable," "final sale" or the like and out-of-print, collectible or pre-owned items cannot be returned or exchanged.

Returns and exchanges to a Borders, Borders Express or Waldenbooks retail store of merchandise purchased from Borders.com may be permitted in certain circumstances. See Borders.com for details.

```
****************              ***
   BORDERS   EWARDS
    MEMBERS ONLY

 COME BACK AND SAVE

      30% OFF
     List Price of
     One Item

     Valid at Borders,
 Tuesday, 8/4 - Sunday, 8/9/09

POS: Enter S1, highight item, S5,
scan barcode, 30%.
```

```
 1 5 9 0 4 3 1 4 0 0 0 0 0 0 0 0 0
```

Returns

Returns of merchandise purchased from a Borders, Borders Express or Waldenbooks retail store will be permitted only if presented in saleable condition accompanied by the original sales receipt or Borders gift receipt within the time periods specified below. Returns accompanied by the original sales receipt must be made within 30 days of purchase and the purchase price will be refunded in the same form as the original purchase. Returns accompanied by the original Borders gift receipt must be made within 60 days of purchase and the purchase price will be refunded in the form of a return gift card.

Exchanges of opened audio books, music, videos, video games, software and electronics will be permitted subject to the same time periods and receipt requirements as above and can be made for the same item only.

Periodicals, newspapers, comic books, food and drink, digital downloads, gift cards, return gift cards, items marked "non-returnable," "final sale" or the like and out-of-print, collectible or pre-owned items cannot be returned or exchanged.

Returns and exchanges to a Borders, Borders Express or Waldenbooks retail store of merchandise purchased from Borders.com may be permitted in certain circumstances. See Borders.com for details.

BORDERS.

Returns

Returns of merchandise purchased from a Borders, Borders Express or Waldenbooks retail store will be permitted only if presented in saleable condition accompanied by the original sales receipt or Borders gift receipt within the time periods specified below. Returns accompanied by the original sales receipt must be made within

International has been run by the Donohoe family for generations; most of the bar staff have the place in their blood. The traditional, no-frills interior with big tables and comfy seats attracts a cross-section of ages. It's also a venue for comedy and live music. (see p 128). *23 Wicklow St.* ☎ *01-677 9250. www. international-bar.com. Map p 114.*

★★ **Kehoe's** The dark wood interior and snug (with its Victorian-era serving hatch and buzzer) has seen more than two centuries of pints being pulled. The front still has the mahogany drawers from its grocery store heritage, and upstairs is like your old auntie's living room. On summer evenings, the after-work and student crowds spill onto the pavements. *9 South St Anne St.* ☎ *01-677 8312. Map p 114.*

★★ **The Library Bar** Sink into your leather armchair, surrounded by groaning bookshelves, wooden floor-boards, and immersed in hush, and forget the city's chaos. The antithesis to Temple Bar frivolities, this is ideal for a relaxing whiskey in front of the roaring log fire on a cold (or even warm) evening. *Central Hotel, Exchequor St.* ☎ *01-679 7302. www.centralhotel.ie. Map p 114.*

★ **The Long Hall** Another fine traditional bar, with little attempt to compete with the Temple Bar super-pubs (i.e., no music or TV). Yes it's long, very long and narrow, with Victorian décor: a pretty relaxing place to show up and join a real cross-section of locals. Friendly staff. *51 South Great Georges St.* ☎ *01-475 1590. Map p 114.*

★ **Market Bar** A former sausage factory inside Georges Street Arcade, this vast high-ceilinged warehouse has been carefully redesigned with red-brick walls and skylights. Funky contemporary art and tall plants add to the style. Come for tapas, a quiet early evening drink, good wine list, and buzzing evenings; with a large heated courtyard. *Fade St.* ☎ *01-613 9094. www.marketbar.ie. Map p 114.*

★★ **McDaid's** This classic old Dublin boozer poured many a pint for literary legends Brendan Behan and Thomas Kavanagh. It's certainly lost nothing of its charm, with its welcoming Victorian interior and dark wood walls, packing locals, students, and visitors into its tiny space. Try for a snug, or perch up at the bar for a friendly chat. *3 Harry St.* ☎ *01-679 4395. Map p 114.*

The former sausage factory and now Market Bar.

★★ Mint Bar A sophisticated cocktail bar in the basement of the Westin Hotel, this is suitable for a quiet intimate drink, probably at the end of a long night (a kind of one-for-the-road with style), or at the start. The cocktail menu is imaginative (albeit pricey) and service, in my experience, better than the more famous Octagon. *The Westin Hotel, Westmoreland St.* ☎ *01-645 1000. www.westin.com/dublin. Map p 114.*

★★ Mulligans Probably the best Guinness in town, and has been since the 1850s, even though James Joyce (a regular) had characters of *Dubliners* drinking hot whiskeys here. Mulligans is for those who appreciate a smooth pint, ornate dusty mirrors, and mahogany snugs immersed in old-time ambience. *Poolbeg St.* ☎ *01-677 5582. www. mulligans.ie. Map p 113.*

★ Ocean Tucked away on Grand Canal Quay, this is frequented by hip youngsters living in the renovated dockland area. Join them on a summer's evening, on a comfy sofa by the window or out on the waterfront terrace. Sip on cocktails and peruse the tempting menu. *1st floor, Millennium Tower, Charlotte Quay Dock.* ☎ *01-668 8862. Map p 113.*

★ Octagon Many come here for the hotel owners, and yes, Bono has been seen once or twice. An eight-sided snug interior with great skylight, it is relatively quiet even when filled with wannabe celebs and rich businessfolk (the drinks are pricey). A great cocktail menu and usually well-made, this isn't the place to order a pint. *Clarence Hotel, 6–8 Wellington Quay.* ☎ *01-407 0800. Map p 114.*

★★ Odeon Once part of the old Harcourt Street Railway Station, the recent conversion sees a huge patio and Art Deco interior. Popular with young folk en route to the adjacent club Tripod, or the post-work crowd letting their hair down with decent wine and food. DJs play house and funk on Saturday nights. Service can be slow. *Harcourt St.* ☎ *01-478 2088. www.odeon.ie. Map p 113.*

★★ O'Donoghue's Although tourists love to visit the place where The Dubliners made their name on the music scene, it's also busy with office-workers who pack into the large heated alleyway. With walls lined with photos of music stars of the past, this is still a place for impromptu trad music sessions. *15 Merrion Row.* ☎ *01-660 7194. www.odonoghues.ie. Map p 113.*

O'Donoghue's sign.

★★ Ryans The Victorian interior has seen the likes of Presidents Clinton, Kennedy. and Bush Snr supping pints, and we agree they made a good choice. Its gorgeous mahogany fittings and old lamps have retained the charm of the one-time gentleman's retreat; luckily no such sexism is in place these days with all punters treated to a fine pint, and food served all day. *28 Parkgate St.* ☎ *01-677 6097. www.fxb restaurants.com. Map p 113.*

★★★ The Schoolhouse Part of the Schoolhouse Hotel, and a school from 1861, its 12m (40-ft) beamed ceilings, deep sofas, and log fires are a treat on a cold evening—though it

Drinking lessons at The Schoolhouse.

also feels a bit like having a tipple in a cavernous church. Informal and lively after work, it's proved a hit with its food, way better than your average pub grub. The garden is a lovely spot in summer, and a peaceful lunchtime spot. *2–8 Northumberland Rd.* ☎ *01-614 4733. www.schoolhouse hotel.com. Map p 113.*

★ **Stag's Head**   Tucked away from the main drag, you can't miss the stag's head mounted proudly on the wall. Decorated in Victoriana with a bar inlaid with Connemara marble, stained-glass windows, and a lovely at-home feel, you'll feel cocooned in here with a decent pint, and joined by an affable mix of students, IFSC workers, afternoon skivers, and locals. *1 Dame Court.* ☎ *01-679 3687. Map p 114.*

★★★ **Wine Cellar**   In the stone-walled basement of the fabulous Fallon & Byrne food emporium (see p 81 and 105), some 350 bottles of wine from 12 countries are on offer with decent food (oysters!) to soak it up. Comfortable, decadent, and cozy, yet reasonably priced; a real find. *11–17 Exchequer St.* ☎ *01-472 1010. www.fallonandbyrne.com. Map p 114.*

DJ Bars

★★ **Anseo**   Pronounced An-Shaw, this slightly leftfield, casually hip and fun place has DJ playing at weekends. Although there's no "official" dance space, those in the mood will get up and boogie where it takes their fancy. *8 Camden St Lower.* ☎ *01-475 1321. Map p 113.*

★ **Bleeding Horse**   A huge, rambling old bar (the original bleed-ing horse allegedly staggered by in 1649) split over three floors, this has a DJ playing on Friday and Saturday nights: old favorites that you can sing along to, rather than needing space to dance. Snug corners and small balconies provide space for small groups to chat (yell) above the music. *25 Camden St.* ☎ *01-475 2705. Map p 113.*

★★ **Dice Bar**   It looks like a Goth hangout, but this black-walled, red-lit bar with bizarre flying spaceman out-side the toilet is a popular DJ bar with a great mixture of music and hip regulars—and no cover charge. With rockabilly on Sundays, blues on Wednesdays, and even a monthly Frank Zappa night, the "dance floor" can get crowded. Off the beaten

Flying spaceman at Dice Bar.

track, it's worth the detour. *79 Queen St.* 📞 *01-872 8622. Map p 113.*

★ **Pravda** With its bizarre Russian-themed décor (murals and nick-nacks) and a world of vodkas, Pravda's live music nights get the twentysomething punters in, and weekends have good DJs playing indie. I love the red leather sofas upstairs, but competition is tight. Renowned for its civilized monthly Latin night and anything-goes weekly King Kong Club open-mic night. *Lower Liffey St.* 📞 *01-874 0090. www.pravda.ie. Map p 113.*

★★ **Sin É** This friendly, studenty pub has a loyal following, with a bonus Liffey view. Relatively new yet with an old-time feel, it's usually a pretty relaxed place (except at weekends) with the back area for regular trad music sessions and weekend DJ sets; a Northside gem. *14–15 Upper Ormond Quay.* 📞 *01-878 7078. Map p 113.*

Clubs

★ **Gaiety Theatre Late Night Club** When the thespians leave, the party-goers arrive. From midnight, Dublin's oldest theater turns into a mega-club with four bars hosting live bands and DJs, usually comprising RnB, Latin, and Hip Hop, plus Northern Soul and live Blues. Its all-night movie theater shows films for clubbers who need a breather. Funky and fun, don't forget to check out the ornate décor before you get too drunk. *South King St.* 📞 *01-677 1717. Map p 114.*

★ **Howl at the Moon** This huge multi-level bar/club draws in a young crowd with DJs playing popular dance tracks, although nothing too techno. There's no cover and no official dress code, which adds an air of non-exclusivity to the place, thankfully. Different areas with varied

décor, some sofas and bar stools make it cozy, plus there's a small outdoor terrace. *Lower Mount St.* 📞 *01-634 5460. www.capitalbars.com. Weds–Sat till late. Map p 113.*

★ **Lilllie's Bordello** Its red walls and sensual décor used to be *the* place to be seen, frequented by local and visiting celebs. Now its impact has worn off, and vaguely smartly dressed non-members will probably get past the discerning doormen, especially earlier in the week. It still has its fair share of poseurs and wannabes, but it's free Sunday to Tues, so give it a go and have a cocktail. *Adam Court, Grafton St.* 📞 *01-679 9204. www.lillies bordello.ie. Free Sun–Tues, Weds €5, Thurs €10, Fri & Sat €15. Map p 114.*

★★ **POD** Leaping onto the club scene in 1993, the venue of the old Harcourt Street railway station sees garage and house in its mandarin-hued lighting and granite walls, with noted house DJs and occasional high-caliber guests including Paul Oakenfold and Boy George. The flagship of this music mecca. (See also *Crawdaddy* in Arts & Entertainment p 130.) *Old Harcourt St Train Station.* 📞 *01-476 3374. www.pod. ie. Wed–Sat from 11pm–2.30am. Cover from €10. Luas: Harcourt Street. Map p 113.*

★★ **Ri-Ra** The Globe's (see p 115) basement has nightly DJs playing, on different nights, a range of R&B, rock, funk, and punk, with Monday's "Strictly Handbag" night given over to 80s and 90s sounds. A chilled out crowd with cozy, dark areas, and general carefree, pose-free attitude. *11 South Great George's St.* 📞 *01-671 1220. www.rira.ie. Mon–Sat 11.30pm–2.30am. €7–€10 cover. Map p 114.*

★ **The Vaults** The basement of Connolly Station houses vaults built in 1846, and the vast stone-walled, high-ceilinged venue with spooky statues is now split off into several bars and clubs. The "Nite Club" is for serious twentysomething techno fans, with local and visiting DJs playing electro house and soul. If that's too scary, enjoy a quiet glass of wine in the main bar in the early evening with city slickers. *Harbourmaster Place, IFSC.* ☎ *01-605 4700. www.thevaults.ie. €10–€30 cover, depending on DJs. Map p 113.*

Gay Bars & Clubs

★ **The Dragon** Featuring a row of camp snugs on one side, elaborate glam lighting, a mezzanine overlooking the dancefloor, and a huge Chinese dragon in the window, Dublin's only dedicated gay club has DJs playing techno, hard house, and pop most nights. The friendly, snappy-dressed crowd love the cocktails (try the Cookie Monster) and flirting galore in the outdoor smoking area. *South Georges St.* ☎ *01-478 1590 www.capitalbars. com. No cover. Map p 114.*

★★ **The George** An institution for Dublin's growing gay community, this longstanding favorite (and The Dragon's big sister) is split into two: the traditional Old Bar is frequented by pint-drinking men of all ages, and the adjacent Dance Bar/Club gets in a young trendy crowd, with weekend DJs, comedy nights every Wednesday, and the unmissable Shirley's Bingo Sundays. *87 South Great Georges St.* ☎ *01-478 2983. www. capitalbars.com. Map p 114.*

Live Music Bars (see also *Arts & Entertainment* p 123)

★★ **Bruxelles** A rock venue for late birds and bikers, with live jazz every Sunday afternoon and bands five nights a week, including rock, indie, and blues. The three bars have two DJs playing rock and indie at weekends, so it's best to order a Belgian beer and check them all out. Open late every night, its huge patio gets packed on summer evenings. If you get late-night munchies, they also serve decent Irish food. *7–8 Harry St.* ☎ *01-677 5362. Map p 114.*

Glam décor at The Dragon.

Live trad Irish music at Cobblestone.

★★★ Cobblestone   This is probably the best place to hang out with locals listening to good Irish music. Head through the shabby exterior to the little wooden-floored interior. If there's a band playing, likely everyone will be drinking Guinness and listing earnestly. It's great fun, friendly, and earthy. *77 North King St, Smithfield.* ☎ *01-872 1799. Live music Mon–Weds 9pm;* Thurs–Sat 7pm; Sun 2pm. No cover. *Luas: Smithfield. Map p 113.*

★★ Hughes Bar   A little rough round the edges (even though it's just behind the Four Courts) but Hughes is renowned for some of the finest trad Irish with musicians pitching up for a session. There are good sounds every night from around 9.30pm, with a haphazard selection of fiddles and pipes, very informal, and unpredictable. *19 Chancery St.* ☎ *01-872 6540. No cover. Map p 113.*

★★ Porterhouse Central
This three-floored informal bar is the flagship of the microbrewery chain and Ireland's largest genuine brewery. Live bands play nightly on a tiny stage (best seen from the top-floor balcony) with bluesy rock on Mondays, local bands midweek, and traditional music sessions at weekends. Don't ask for Guinness; ask the bar staff what they recommend according to your taste (my favorite is Oyster). Look out for the old brewing memorabilia, including the huge brass pot on the top floor. *16–18 Parliament St.* ☎ *01-679 8847. www. porterhousebrewco.com. No cover. Map p 114.* ●

Original brewing tools at Porterhouse Central.

The Best Arts & Entertainment

Arts & Entertainment Best Bets

Best for **Swinging Your Partners**
★★ Comhaltas Ceoltoiri Eireann, *32 Belgrave Square, Monkstown* (p 129)

Best **Experimental Dance**
★★ Project Arts Centre, *39 East Essex St., Temple Bar* (p 134)

Best **Irish Sporting Experience**
★★★ Croke Park, *Jones's Rd* (p 132)

Best for **Race Goers**
★★ Leopardstown Race Course, *Leopardstown* (p 132)

Best for **Glam Premiers**
★★ The Savoy, *17 Upper O'Connell St.* (p 129)

Best for **a Random Flutter**
★★★ Shelbourne Park Greyhound Stadium, *Shelbourne Park* (p 132)

Best for **Sax Fans**
★★ Bleu Note Bar & Club, *61–62 Capel St.* (p 130)

Best **Beckett Plays**
★★★ Gate Theatre, *1 Cavendish Row* (p 134)

Best **Concert Acoustics**
★★★ National Concert Hall, *Earlsfort Terrace* (p 127)

Best **Pub Comedy Night**
★★★ The International, *23 Wicklow St.* (p 128)

Best **Specialist Kid's Venue**
★★ Ark, *11a Eustace St., Temple Bar* (p 127)

Best **Art Gallery recitals**
★★ Hugh Lane Gallery, *Parnell Square North* (p 127)

Best for **Hard-Core Rock Fans**
★★★ Voodoo Lounge, *39–40 Arran Quay* (p 131)

Best **Arthouse Films**
★★ IFI, *6 Eustace St.* (p 129)

Best **Daytime Drama**
★★ Bewleys Café Theatre, *78–79 Grafton St.* (p 133)

Opera Ireland performing La Traviata.

North Dublin Arts & Entertainment

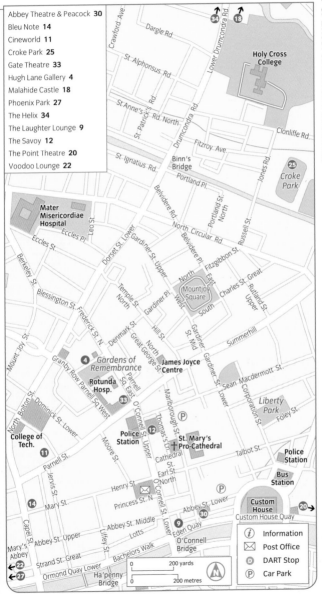

South Dublin Arts & Entertainment

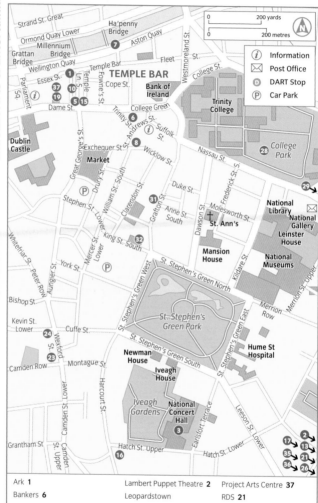

0		200 yards	
0		200 metres	

ⓘ	Information
✉	Post Office
Ⓓ	DART Stop
Ⓟ	Car Park

Ark **1**	Lambert Puppet Theatre **2**	Project Arts Centre **37**
Bankers **6**	Leopardstown	RDS **21**
Bewley's Café Theatre **31**	Racecourse **26**	Shelbourne Park **29**
Button Factory **15**	Marley Park **17**	The International **8**
Comhaltas Ceoltóirí Éireann **13**	Mill Theatre **35**	University of Dublin
CrawDaddy **16**	National Concert Hall **3**	Cricket Club **28**
Gaiety Theatre **32**	Olympia Theatre **19**	The Village **24**
Ha'penny Bridge Inn **7**	Opera Theatre Company **5**	Whelans **23**
IFI **10**	Pavilion **36**	

Arts & Entertainment **A to Z**

Children's Entertainment

★★ Ark The lovely Children's Cultural Centre hosts programs, shows, festivals, and exhibitions for kids of all ages, such as the wonderful *Century of Toys* exhibition in 2007, with artists and performers from Ireland and around the world. Most events are during the summer, and weekends year-round. *11a Eustace St, Temple Bar.* ☎ *01-670 7788. www.ark.ie. Tickets free–€10. Map p 126. (See also p 31.)*

★★ Lambert Puppet Theatre

The family-run theater with all puppets hand-made, puts on popular fairy-tales such as *Jack and the Beanstalk* and *Little Red Riding Hood* and more edgy tales like Oscar Wilde's *The Selfish Giant*. Performances are held most weekends throughout the year. *Clifton Lane, Monkstown.* ☎ *01-280 0974. www. lambertpuppettheatre.com. Tickets €10–€13. DART: Salthill & Monkstown. Map p 126. (See also p 31.)*

Classical Music & Opera

★★ Hugh Lane Gallery This gorgeous gallery hosts **Sundays at Noon**, free recitals among the Impressionist paintings every Sunday with specially commissioned works, concerts coinciding with major exhibitions, and visiting international performers. Concerts are informal, free, and attract all ages. *Charlemont House, Parnell Square North.* ☎ *01-222 5550. www. hughlane.ie. Concerts Oct–June. Map p 125.*

★★ National Concert Hall

Sitting on the edge of Iveagh Gardens (see p 89), the purpose-built hall is regarded as one of Ireland's (and Europe's) best for live performances. The Resident RTE National Symphony Orchestra gives weekly recitals, with concerts every night and most lunchtimes of Irish and international artists and orchestras: think popular classics rather than anything too high-brow. *Earlsfort Terrace.* ☎ *01-417 0077. www. nch.ie. Tickets €10–€80. Map p 126.*

★ Opera Ireland Performing four operas in winter and spring seasons at the Gaiety Theatre, Opera Ireland put on the classics (*Turandot* and *Marriage of Figaro*) in

Advance Tickets & Listings

For the latest concert, theater, cinema, and event listings, pick up a copy of **The Ticket** (www.ireland.com/theticket) a weekly guide free with Friday's **Irish Times**. Venues around Temple Bar have free copies of fortnightly **The Event Guide** (www.eventguide.ie) and look out in bars and cafés for the tabloid-sized **Totally Dublin** and magazine **InDublin** (www.indublin.ie), both free. Buy tickets from **Tickets.ie** (☎ 087-263 3920; www.tickets.ie, www.ticketmaster.ie, **Celtic Note** (see p 84) (Nassau St), **Centra Temple Bar** (45–46 Wellington Quay), **Dublin Tourism** (Suffolk St), and **Ticketron** (Jervis St Shopping Centre & Stephen's Green Shopping Centre).

Performance at the National Concert Hall.

2007, but is also renowned for its Irish premiers of contemporary opera. Top names such as Pavarotti, Carreras, and Domingo have been guest soloists. ☎ *01-478 6041. www.operaireland.com. Tickets €20–€90. (For tickets and map, see Gaiety Theatre.)*

★ **Opera Theatre Company** Operating on a small budget, this friendly crew has toured the country giving performances since 1986 in a whole host of venues, including theaters and churches. Even more unusual, they performed Beethoven's Fidelio at Kilmainham Gaol in 2007. Apart from the classics, it also performs new operas by

Comedy improv at The International.

Irish composers. *Office: Temple Bar Music Centre, Curved St. ☎ 01-679 4962. www.opera.ie. Map p 126.*

Comedy

★ **Bankers** This cozy basement in a city center bar hosts hit-and-miss **Stand-Up at the Bankers** with Irish comics on Thursday and Saturday, and the **Comedy Improv** with resident troupe the Craic Pack on Wednesday, and their biggest night, Friday. Avoid the front row seats unless you don't mind being picked on. *16 Trinity St. ☎ 01-679 3697. www.bankerscomedyclub.com. Doors open 9pm; show 9.30pm. Tickets €10. Map p 126.*

★ **Ha'penny Bridge Inn** This popular quayside bar puts on some sort of entertainment every night. The Battle of the Axe (upstairs at the Ha'penny), puts on an open-mic night for all sorts to put themselves in the firing line of the discerning public, while Thursday is comedy night, with stand-up, improv and sketch. *42 Wellington Quay, Temple Bar. ☎ 01-677 0616. Doors open 9pm; show 9.30pm. Tickets €7. www. battleoftheaxe.com. Map p 126.*

★★★ **The International** The comedy nights upstairs at this friendly bar host improv comedy on

Monday (be prepared to contribute), and stand-up comedy with established locals nightly except Tuesday. The comedy has been going strong for more than a decade, and is still drawing in a lovely crowd; my personal favourite. *23 Wicklow St.* 01-679 3697. *www.the international comedyclub.com. Doors open 8.30pm; show 9 pm. Tickets €10. Map p 126.*

★ **The Laughter Lounge** No pub backroom here; open after major refurbishment, this slick venue hosts shows with well-established stand-up acts every Thurs–Sat, with four comedians from Ireland and overseas. Tuck into finger food or a three-course meal before the show. DJs and late bars keep the party going after you've finished chuckling. *Basement, 4–8 Eden Quay.* 01-878 3003. *www.laughterlounge.com. Doors open 7pm; show 8.30–11pm. Tickets €25–€30. Map p 125.*

Irish Traditional Music & Dance

★★ **Comhaltas Ceoltoiri Eireann** This cultural center to promote Irish traditional music takes its music seriously though its informal music sessions four nights a week are good fun. Half the charm is never quite knowing who's turning up. Put your newfound rhythm into practice at the Friday night Ceilidh, complete with caller, live musicians, and dancers who know their sets from their steps and jigs. Forget *Riverdance*, just jump in. *32 Belgrave Square, Monkstown.* 01-280 0295. *www.comhaltas.ie. Tickets (Ceilidh) €10; music sessions Tues & Weds free; Fri & Sat €3. DART: Seapoint. Map 126.*

Movies

★ **Cineworld** One of the largest and most popular movie theaters in the city center, with 17 large screens, comfortable seats, and a host of refreshments plus the rare luxury of a licensed bar. Most movies are new releases and blockbusters, plus the occasional Bollywood and kung-fu flick. *Parnell St.* 1520-880444. *www.cineworld.ie. Tickets €5.40–€9.70. Map p 125.*

★★ **IFI** The national Irish Film Institute has regular screenings of arthouse, foreign, and vintage movies, as well as housing the Irish Film Archive and library. It shows several different films every day, plus puts on festivals such as the "Annual Polish Film Festival". It's a lovely venue with a bar and restaurant. *6 Eustace St.* 01-679 5744. *www.ifi.ie. Tickets €8–€11. Map p 126.*

★ **The Savoy** Dublin's oldest movie theater has been screening movies since 1929, seen countless changes, and is now a slick multi-screen venue. A recent €2m refurbishment restored the original interior features, and the marble-floored foyer and chandeliers make it the location of choice for many Irish premiers: The famous number one auditorium with 780 seats still has the original red drapes on the

Sax appeal at Bleu Note.

Dublin's Cultural Festivals

All things turn green for the week-long **St Patrick's Day** revelry, with parades galore and ample liquid refreshment (from March 13; www.stpatricksfestival.ie) followed by the more sedate **Handel's Messiah Festival** on the anniversary of its world premier (13 April). Contemporary dancers from around the world take to various venues during April's **Dublin Dance Festival** (☎ 01-679 0524; www.dance festivalireland.ie). The first fortnight in May showcases gay contributors to the theater, past and present, in the **Dublin Gay Theatre Festival** (www.gaytheatre.ie) and majestic tallships come sailing by in the **Docklands Maritime Festival** (☎ 01-818 3300; www.dublin docklands.ie). Temple Bar's bohemian edge is spotlighted during the summer's three-month **Temple Bar Diversions Festival** starting in June, (☎ 01-677 2255; www.templebar.ie) from outdoor film screenings to live opera. Head for the coast and Dún Laoghaire's **Festival of World Culture** in August. International music, theater, and cabaret crams into a frantic fortnight in September's **Dublin Fringe Festival** (☎ 01-677 8511; www.fringefest.com), followed by the **Dublin Theatre Festival** (☎ 01-677 8439; www.dublintheatrefestival.com), the world's oldest English-speaking festival.

screen. *17 Upper O'Connell St.* ☎ *0818 776 776. www.omniplex.ie. Tickets €7–€9. Map p 125.*

Pop, Rock & Jazz

★★★ Bleu Note Bar & Club
Dublin's only dedicated venue for live jazz is not just for hard-core jazz heads. A relaxed friendly venue with a surprisingly mixed crowd, Fridays and Saturdays have acoustic live jazz in the basement, with Big Band sounds every Monday on the 1st floor. There's also salsa, soul, and funk from local bands, and late opening. *61–62 Capel St.* ☎ *01-878 3371. www.bleunoteclub.com. Thurs & Sun free, €5–€12 cover. Map p 125.*

★★ Button Factory This is the new name for the refurbished Temple Bar Music Factory, with live concerts most nights between Weds and Sat, ranging from international names (The Damned, Bad Manners) to local bands. Still a little, grubby venue (even since the smoking ban), the old balcony has now doubled in size with a new bar and seating with a stage view. For real music fans, it retains an informal, studently feel. *Curved St, Temple Bar.* ☎ *01-670 9202. www.tbmc.ie. Most tickets via City Discs (next door), www.tickets.ie or www.ticketmaster.ie. Map p 126.*

★★ CrawDaddy A live music venue with a capacity of 300 (part of the huge Pod venue), and with an eclectic range of performers most nights. CrawDaddy is spread over two floors: the balcony is reserved tiered seating and the 1st floor level is lively standing room only. With a homely ambience, great acoustics and lighting, recent performers include Courtney Pine, Youssou N'Dour, and Ice T. The adjacent **Lobby Bar** is relaxed for pre- or post-gig drinks. (See also **Pod**, *Best*

Nightlife p 120.) *Old Harcourt Station, Harcourt St.* ☎ *01-662 4305.* *www.pod.ie. Cover from approx €7. Map p 126.*

★ **Malahide Castle** A recent addition to the supergroup venue, the huge grounds of the 12th-century castle (see *Day Trips & Excursions p 147*) is expanding its number of concerts in the summer months after a successful start that included thousands of Pink fans braving the rain for the gig. A lovely location in sight of the castle. *Malahide Castle. DART: Malahide. Map p 125.*

★ **Marlay Park** A huge suburban park spanning over 121 hectares (300 acres), and venue to supergroups who are likely to attract around 30,000 fans. In 2007, Peter Gabriel, The Who, and Nine Inch Nails did just that. Tickets via agencies in advance. *Marley Park, Rathfarnam. Map p 126.*

★ **Olympia Theatre** This one-time music hall now offers its ornate walls to the occasional play, but more often big names (albeit safe bets) in the music scene such as Don McLean and Gilbert O'Sullivan. Its gorgeous 19th-century stained-glass canopy outside was finally repaired in 2007. *72 Dame St.* ☎ *01-679 3323.* *www.mcd.ie/venues. Map p 126.*

★★ **RDS** The Royal Dublin Society, founded in 1731, was set up to promote the arts, industry, and science, and is now a multi-purpose venue hosting concerts, shows, conferences, and even the Horse of the Year Show. With retracting roof and flexible seating, it holds 4,000 in the Main Hall and 900 in the Concert Hall. Acts in recent years include U2, Bryan Adams, and Luciano Pavarotti, plus two Eurovision Song Contests. *Ballsbridge.* ☎ *01-668 0866. www.rds.ie. Map p 126.*

★★ **The Point Theatre** Ireland's mega venue: from Disney on Ice to Pavarotti to Riverdance at the 1994 Eurovision Song Contest. The Point on the North Wall Quay will reopen after its mammoth makeover in late 2008. Before its expansion the capacity was 8,500, so be prepared for some high-octane gigs, ballets, and musicals from London's West End. A half-hour walk from the city center. *North Wall Quay.* ☎ *01-676 6144. www.thepointdublin.com. Bus 53A. Map p 125.*

★★ **The Village** Over two floors, a band plays nightly upstairs, followed by resident DJs Thursday to Saturday nights. The bar downstairs (a comfortable earthy place like a student bar that people don't want to grow out of) has decent food. Sundays you can see one of Dublin's most popular nights: a unique night of rock-and-roll karaoke called **Songs of Praise**. *26 Wexford St.* ☎ *01-475 8555. www.thevillage venue.com. Map p 126.*

★★ **Voodoo Lounge** Part-owned by Huey from Fun Lovin' Criminals, this cavernous bar with deep red ceilings and voodoo-esque trinkets is known as the "21st century

The Voodoo Lounge.

rock garden" for its decent gigs. Early in the week sees local indie bands (free), and Thursday to Sunday the tempo (and sound levels) rises for decent punk, metal, ska, and reggae bands. *39–40 Arran Quay.* ☎ *01-873 6013. Thurs–Sun cover €10–€20. Map p 125.*

★★ **Whelans** A sociable wooden-floored bar over two floors sees a live band every night, showcasing local Irish talent and showing off international stars, including folk, rock, indie, and roots (Nick Cave and Christy Moore have played here). The combination is a winner, and recent extensions indicate its popularity. Look out for the Stone Man statue. *25 Wexford St.* ☎ *01-478 0766. www.whelanslive.com. Cover charge for gigs varies. Map p 126.*

Spectator Sports

★★★ **kids Croke Park** Immerse yourself in local sporting culture at a hurling match (the world's fastest field sport) or Gaelic football, at the HQ of the Gaelic Athletic Association, 80,000-seat stadium "the Croker." Fiercely partisan yet non-segregated stands mean a good-natured, noisy, high-octane day out, for kids of all ages. The domestic seasons both run

Cheering on the 'Dubs' at Croke Park.

every weekend from April till September but for big matches, and the finals in September especially if the "Dubs" are playing, legitimate tickets are hard to get. If the sport inspires you, make sure you visit the **GAA Museum** (see p 49) inside. *Jones's Rd.* ☎ *01-865 8657. Tickets from www.ticketmaster.ie., www.gaa.ie., www.crokepark.ie. Admission: €10–€40. Map p 125.*

★★ **Leopardstown Racecourse** Built in 1888 and modeled on England's Sandown Racecourse, suburban Leopards-town with views of Killiney Hill is one of Europe's best, with year-round racing of flat and national hunt courses. Names in the man-and-beast Hall of Fame include Pat Eddery and Nijinsky. Racing experts will appreciate the history; the uninitiated (like me) will love the buzz and "skill" of putting a couple of euros on a horse with a funky name. *Leopardstown.* ☎ *01-289 0500. www.leopardstown.com. Admission: €15–€30. Luas: Sandyford. Map p 126.*

★★ **Phoenix Park** This mammoth urban park has a long history of sports fields, and summer weekends are best to see them in full flow. Try and get to see a polo match. *(See Best of Outdoors p 93.)*

★★ **Shelbourne Park** The speedy greyhounds provide a fun and cheap night out (providing you don't go overboard with the betting) in a newly improved stadium, close to the center. Eat at **Dobbins at the Park** and study the form, although I'm still wondering if it's skill or luck that brings winnings. Weekends have a livelier crowd; get there early for the Irish Greyhound Derby in September, with prize money of more than €300,000. *Shelbourne Park.* ☎ *01-668 3502. www.igb.ie. Races Weds, Thurs & Sat night from 7pm. Admission: €10. Map p 126.*

Let off the leash at Shelbourne Park.

★★ University of Dublin Cricket Club

The Trinity College cricket ground is picturesque, with the "Pav" bar on the boundary, and sunny weekends bring students out in force who might not be cricket fans but nonetheless know that it's a wonderful way of appreciating the venue. There are several teams within the club, including women's teams, and the season runs from April to August. *Trinity College, College Green.* ☎ *01-896 1000. Map p 126. (See Trinity College p 38, bullet* ⑧*.)*

Theaters & Venues

Abbey Founded in 1904 by WB Yeats, this was the first state-subsidized theater in the English-speaking world. A nursery for many Irish playwrights, it went bankrupt in 2004, but a new management at the helm has kept Ireland's best-known theater going, performing classics, such as Arthur Miller's *The Crucible* in 2007. **The Peacock**, under the Abbey's foyer, is a great little venue for new plays and contemporary classic drama. *26 Lower Abbey St.* ☎ *01-878 7222. Tickets prices vary. www.abbeytheatre.ie. Map p 125.*

★★★ Bewley's Café Theatre

A play, a bowl of soup, and a small audience sitting cozily at wooden tables, this charming venue in the old Oriental Room hosts lunchtime drama. Perfect to drop by while shopping or sightseeing and watch a short play, with a late lunch included in the ticket price. *3rd floor, Bewley's, 78–79 Grafton St.* ☎ *086 878 4001. www.bewleyscafetheatre.com. Ticket €14. Map p 126.*

★★ Gaiety Theatre

Although Dublin's longest-established theater, you won't find much high-brow dramatics here. After a huge refurbishment, it hosts mega-musicals and sell-out shows such as *Riverdance* (the first production since reopening) plus London's West End tourist shows such as *Joseph* and *Blood Brothers*. **Opera Ireland** also performs here.

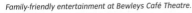

Family-friendly entertainment at Bewleys Café Theatre.

South King St. ☎ 01-677 1717. www.
gaietytheatre.ie. Tickets €22–€55.
Map p 126.

★★ **Gate Theatre** A Dublin
landmark (in both the architectural
and theatrical sense) this opulent
building, once part of the Rotunda
Hospital, brought European and
American avant-garde theater to
Dublin when it opened in 1928. With
longstanding connections to Samuel
Beckett—it recently performed all
19 of his plays—and Brian Friel, it
takes part in many international festivals. A new wing, providing much-
needed facilities, was completed in
2008. *1 Cavendish Row.* ☎ 01-874
4045. www.gate-theatre.ie. Tickets
€25–€30. Map p 125.

★ **Mill Theatre** Nothing historical
about this venue; the 220-seater Mill
is part of the new mega-mall Dundrum Town Centre and opened in
2006. It kicked off with contemporary
productions by Irish, American, and
British companies, plus amateur theater groups, a One-Act Festival, children's shows, and music events. With
decent facilities and restaurants
close by, it's all pretty informal.
Although out in the suburbs, it's easy
to get to. *Dundrum Town Centre.*
☎ 01-296 9340. www.milltheatre.
com. Tickets €10–€20. Luas:
Balally. Map p 126.

★ **Pavilion** A con-
temporary space
out in the
coastal sub-
urbs, this is
the main venue of the Dublin Theatre
Festival and the Festival of World Cultures, and producer of the International Children's Theatre Festival. A
bright space with excellent theater
bar and restaurant, it has a busy
schedule year-round and takes in
touring companies, plus ballet and
contemporary dance; a lovely way to
end a day out to the coast. *Marine
Rd, Dun Laoghaire.* ☎ 01-231 2929.
www.paviliontheatre.ie. Tickets
€10–€30. DART: Dun Laoghaire.
Map p 126.

★ **Project Arts Centre** Temple
Bar's cultural jewel, Project showcases contemporary dance, theater,
and visual arts mainly with Irish
artists. Still sticking to its principles
of nurturing emerging talent—the
likes of U2 and Neil Jordan started
out here—come for experimental
cutting-edge works, rather than
blockbuster classics. Its upstairs bar,
especially, appeals to an eclectic
arty crowd, especially its upstairs
bar. *39 East Essex St, Temple Bar.*
☎ 01-881 9613. www.project.ie.
Map p 126.

★ **The Helix** This venue is
located in Dublin College University's campus and recent productions include *The Nutcracker* by St
Peter's Ballet Theatre, *La Traviata*
by Rostov State Opera, and the
musical *Philadelphia*, plus children's
productions in the annual Fizz Fest.
With its wide variety in cutting-edge,
contemporary design, keep a look-
out for some surprising stars in
overseas theater, opera, and dance
companies. Good for children's
shows. *DCU, Collins Ave, Glasnevin.*
☎ 01-700 7000. www.thehelix.ie.
Tickets €10–€50. Bus 4, 11, 13.
Map p 125. ●

Projects Arts Centre in Temple Bar.

Lodging Best Bets

Best **Wow-Factor Lounge**
★★★ Number 31 $$$$ *31 Leeson Close* (p 144)

Best **Value for Families**
★★ Bewleys $$ *Merrion Rd, Ballsbridge* (p 140)

Best **Hip Boutique Hotel**
★★★ Dylan $$$$$ *Eastmoreland Place* (p 141)

Best **Kid's Swimming Pool**
★★★ Camden Court Hotel $$ *Lower Camden St.* (p 140)

Best **Hedonists' Party Pad**
★★ The Clarence $$$$ *6–8 Wellington Quay* (p 141)

Best **Newcomer**
★★ Radisson SAS Royal $$$ *Golden Lane* (p 145)

Best **In-House Art Gallery**
★★★ Merrion Hotel $$$$ *Upper Merrion St.* (p 144)

Best for **Scholarly Sleeping**
★★ Trinity College $$ *College Green* (p 146)

Most **Dramatic Exterior**
★ Schoolhouse Hotel $$$ *2–8 Northumberland Rd* (p 145)

Best **Dublin Treasure**
★★★ The Shelbourne $$$$$ *27 St Stephen's Green* (p 145)

Best **Value Northsider**
★★★ Comfort Inn $$$ *Smithfield Village* (p 141)

Best **Suburban Luxury**
★★★ Four Seasons $$$$$ *Simmonscourt Rd, Ballsbridge* (p 142)

Best **Cheap Apartment**
★★ Kingfisher $$ *166 Parnell St.* (p 143)

Best **Design Chic**
★★ Morrison Hotel $$$$$ *Ormond Quay* (p 144)

Best **Value Penthouse**
★★ Herbert Park $$$ *Ballsbridge* (p 143)

Best **Garden Terrace View**
★★ Fitzwilliam $$$$ *St Stephen's Green* (p 142)

Best **Temple Bar Cheapie**
★★ Harding Hotel $$ *Copper Alley, Fishamble St.* (p 143)

Best **Live Music**
★★ The Westbury $$$$$ *Grafton St.* (p 146)

Best **Use of a Bank**
★★ Westin $$$$ *College Green, Westmoreland St.* (p 146)

Best **Mural**
★ Park Inn $$ *Smithfield Village* (p 144)

Best **Historic Landmark**
★★ The Gresham $$$$ *23 Upper O'Connell St.* (p 142)

Chief O'Neil mural at Park Inn.

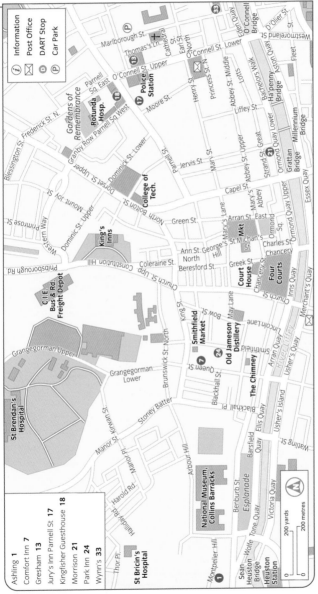

137

Lodging Best Bets

Dublin Lodging

Legend:
- ⓘ Information
- ☒ Post Office
- Ⓓ DART Stop
- Ⓟ Car Park

Lodging list:

- Ashling **1**
- Comfort Inn **7**
- Gresham **13**
- Jury's Inn Parnell St **17**
- Kingfisher Guesthouse **18**
- Morrison **21**
- Park Inn **24**
- Wynn's **33**

South Dublin Lodging

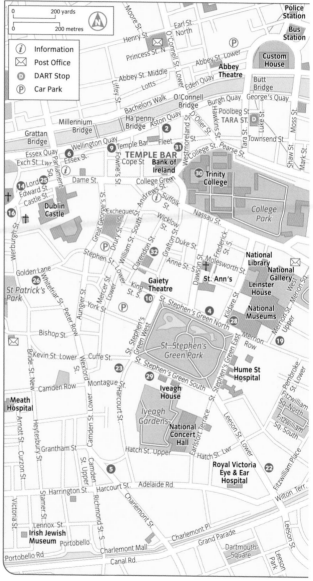

0 — 200 yards
0 — 200 metres

- (i) Information
- (⊠) Post Office
- (D) DART Stop
- (P) Car Park

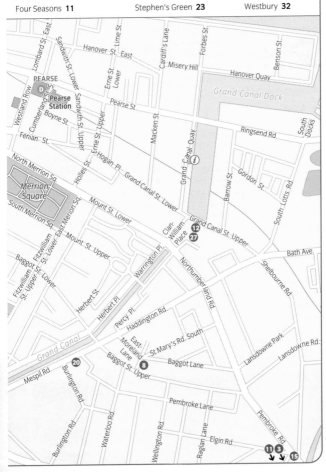

Dublin Lodging **A to Z**

★ **kids Ashling** This Best Western hotel offers average price, clean, serene rooms near Phoenix Park—so a little way from the center but a footstep away from a tram stop. Decent rooms are spacious with décor that wouldn't win style awards but there's nothing too outrageous. Conference and meeting rooms will appeal to the business traveller, and wonderful Ryan's bar (see p 118) is just down the road. *Parkgate St.* ☎ *01-677 2324. www. ashlinghotel.ie. 150 units. €125–€155 w/breakfast AE, DC, MC, V. Luas: Museum. Map p 137.*

★ **Aston** Located right on Aston Quay, this bright and breezy little hotel is all blue and yellow walls, simply furnished and with a small lounge area, and friendly young staff. Lower floor rooms facing the river may have the view, but will be noisy. Most rooms are triple, and family rooms are good value. *7–9 Aston Quay.* ☎ *01-677 9300. www. aston-hotel.com. 27 units. Doubles €90–€180. AE, DC, MC, V. Map p 138.*

★★ **Bewleys** Great value for families, Bewley's offers the same room rates regardless of availability or number of people. But it lacks charisma: rooms are safely and predictably furnished, all with double and single beds. For something extra, ask for a room with a tower view. The exterior is impressive, built from an 1800s Masonic orphanage; check out the entrance mosaic floor. Although suburban, it's only a short bus ride into town. *Merrion Rd, Ballsbridge.* ☎ *01-668 1111. www.bewleyshotels.com. 304 units. Doubles €119. AE, DC, MC, V. Map p 138.*

★ **Brownes** Since 1712 it's been an Earl's townhouse and a Gentlemen's Club, and now it's a seductive little Georgian boutique hotel with just 11 rooms, and so an at-home feel. Rooms can be on the small side, with the best view overlooking St Stephen's Green. Ornate plasterwork on the ceilings and staircases retains its old-world charm. *22 St Stephen's Green.* ☎ *01-638 3939. www.steinhotels.com/brownes. 11 units. Doubles €180–€250. AE, DC, MC, V. Map p 138.*

★★★ **Camden Court Hotel** Recently refurbished rooms are comfortable and simply furnished in strong colors, with all the trimmings including plasma screen TVs. Quieter rooms overlook the courtyard, and there are large family rooms. Not the most fashionable part of town, but it's safe, busy, and a short walk to the

Great pool at Camden Court Hotel.

"Subject to Availability"

It's usually difficult to get a top hotel to quote a general price for a standard double. Many can quote a "rack rate" but in practice this is rarely used, making it hard for you to plan and budget accordingly. Only when you quote a specific date can you get a room rate quoted, as rates vary alarmingly, often from day to day. Unless you're visiting Dublin for a specific occasion, bear in mind that during major sports events (international rugby, GAA semi finals) and concerts, prices leap up and availability down. The flip side is that for luxury hotels, their own websites often have good deals during off-peak times, especially at weekends. Medium and lower priced hotels usually have fixed rates, higher at weekends. Wherever you stay, it always pays to book as far ahead as possible!

center. Rare luxuries include the kids' swimming pool plus a 16m (17.5 yard) adults' pool, sauna, steamroom, and gym. Brilliant value. *Lower Camden St.* ☎ *01-475 9666. www. camdencourthotel.com. 246 units. Doubles €125–€185 w/breakfast. AE, DC, MC, V. Luas: Harcourt. Map p 138.*

★★ **The Clarence** Owned by Bono but there's no rock-star exuberance here, preferring understated elegance with unfussy furnishings, neutral tones, and homely comforts in a mid-19th-century building with an Art Deco interior. Rooms have light oak furniture, some with a Liffey view and balcony, and world radio via a multimedia center. The moneyed people party in the pricey Penthouse (where U2 shot the "Beautiful Day" video) running the entire length of the hotel. *6–8 Wellington Quay.* ☎ *01-407 0800. www.theclarence.ie. 49 units. Doubles €180–€350. AE, DC, MC, V. Map p 138.*

★★★ **kids** **Comfort Inn** Right on the cobbled square in fast-developing Smithfield, and a short walk to the Liffey, the big bright rooms go the extra mile. Rooms are designed with strong colors and unfussy décor

with bathtub, power shower, and free broadband; most have a double and single bed and so are good for families. Quiet location, great value, and very popular. *Smithfield Village.* ☎ *01-485 0900. www.comfortinn dublincity.com. 92 units. Doubles €90–€230. AE, DC, MC, V. Map p 137.*

★★★ **Dylan** With decadent deep red carpets, bold gilded silver mirrors, and strongly designed headboards that should be in an art gallery, this slick new boutique hotel was built in a Victorian nurses' home. Popular with the stylish, beautiful people, and in a quiet part of town a short walk from the center, the hotel

The boutique style Dylan Hotel.

also offers fantastic bathrooms, and some pricey extras. *Eastmoreland Place.* ☎ *01-660 3000. www.dylan.ie. 44 units. Doubles from €240. AE, DC, MC, V. Map p 138.*

★ **kids** **Eliza Lodge** With a guesthouse feel and friendly service, the Eliza Lodge has simple and light rooms, some of them a bit pokey and most with a fantastic Liffey view. It's worth paying a little extra for a Penthouse room with balcony and huge bay windows. It can get noisy. *23/24 Wellington Quay.* ☎ *01-671 8044. www.dublinlodge. com. 18 units. Doubles €130–€190 w/breakfast. AE, MC, V. Map p 138.*

★★ **kids** **Fitzwilliam** Designed by Sir Terence Conran, this hip yet carefully styled luxury hotel has a contemporary feel. Rooms are unfussy with clean lines, soft creams, and chocolate browns, and bathrooms have an amazing power shower. With an enviable central location overlooking St Stephen's Green, the garden terrace suites have fantastic views and balconies with heated lamps. Clientele includes hip families and business travelers. *St Stephen's Green.* ☎ *01-478 7000. www.fitzwilliamhotel.com. 139 units. Doubles €225–€400. AE, DC, MC, V. Map p 138.*

The Fitzwilliam, St Stephen's Green.

★★★ **Four Seasons** Located in a peaceful area just a short ride from the city center, this huge hotel, with stunning exterior, offers all the Four Seasons brand excellence you can expect. Rooms are classic and well furnished. The imposing foyer is a curious mix of antique clocks and ornate carpet yet contemporary artwork, which sets the tone. The hotel also boasts a decent spa with swimming pool, plus acres of space for lounges and terraces. *Simmonscourt Rd, Ballsbridge.* ☎ *01-665 4000. www.fourseasons.com. 197 units. Doubles €295–€445. AE, DC, MC, V. Map p 138.*

★★ **kids** **Grand Canal Hotel** Popular with business travelers, it's a short walk from the center and next to the Grand Canal and DART coastal train. Well-furnished, the comfortable rooms are spacious and quiet, with extras such as free WiFi throughout and ice machines on every floor. Balcony rooms boast amazing views. *Grand Canal Street Upper.* ☎ *01-646 1000. www. grandcanalhotel.com. 142 units. Doubles €110–€230. AE, DC, MC, V. Map p 138.*

★★ **kids** **The Gresham** A landmark on busy O'Connell Street, the Gresham has been around since

1817 but its recent refurb brings it right up to date. Rooms are different sizes, and most bathrooms are small, but all have understated elegance and decent facilities such as large writing desk, WiFi, and plasma TV. You can splash out with the opulent two-bedroom Elizabeth Taylor Suite. Triple-glazing helps keep the street noise out. *23 Upper O'Connell St.* ☎ *01-874 6881. www.gresham-hotels.com. 298 units. Doubles €150–€350. AE, DC, MC, V. Map p 137.*

★★ kids **Harding Hotel** On Dublin's oldest street, near Temple Bar's party scene, the Harding is one of the best budget hotels around. The decent-sized simple rooms were refurbished in 2007 and all have fridge, kettle, small TV, and free WiFi. It might not be luxury, but it's decent value, with huge triple and family rooms. *Copper Alley, Fishamble St.* ☎ *01-679 6500. www.harding hotel.ie. 52 units. Doubles €90–€125, w/breakfast. AE, MC, V. Metro: Sagrada Família. Map p 138.*

★★ kids **Herbert Park** A quiet retreat outside the center, the Herbert Park is popular with business travelers, young families, or those wanting some peace. The huge marble foyer is a little soulless, but rooms are large and elegant, and with contemporary decor, widescreen TV, writing desk, and broadband. For a little extra you can pay for the view onto the 20 hectares (48 acres) of park, with a kids' playground. The penthouse is good value. *Ballsbridge.* ☎ *01-667 2200. www.herbertparkhotel.ie. 153 units. Doubles €125–€250. AE, DC, MC, V. Map p 138.*

★ **Jury's Inn Christchurch** Straightforward simple rooms bang opposite Christ Church Cathedral, make this ideal for sightseeing if not for a quiet night (request upper

Sink into the drawing room at the Merrion.

floors at the back for peace, front for views). The rooms are decently furnished in slightly dated décor, but neat nonetheless, and there are some family rooms. Bathrooms are on the small side. *Christchurch Place.* ☎ *01-454 0000. www.jurysdoyle. com. 182 units. Doubles €100–€160. AE, DC, MC, V. Map p 138.*

★ kids **Jury's Inn Parnell Street** A few seconds from the north end of O'Connell Street, this reliable Irish chain is good value and safe, if not particularly stylish. Most rooms have a double and single bed, and so are good value for families. It's not in the most fashionable end of town, but isn't too noisy at night. *Moore St Plaza, Parnell St.* ☎ *01-878 4900. www.jurysdoyle.com. 253 units. Doubles €100–€160. AE, DC, MC, V. Map p 137.*

★ **Kingfisher Guesthouse & Apartments** A decent budget option, just a few minutes from O'Connell Street, most of the simple rooms have a tiny kitchenette, with microwave and fridge. The apartments, in three different locations, are a better bargain, with living room and kitchen for roughly the same price: good value but don't expect luxury. *Guesthouse: 166 Parnell St.* ☎ *01-872 8732.*

The Westin's huge Atrium.

www.kingfisherdublin.com. 32 units (inc guesthouse & apartments). Doubles €90–€110, apartment €55 per person. AE, MC, V. Map p 137.

★★ **Merrion Hotel** Gorgeous Georgian luxury: created from elegant townhouses—including the Duke of Wellington's birthplace—superbly restored and renovated, its rooms have the finest linen, antiques and high sash windows. Walls are laden with a fantastic private collection of 19th- and 20th-century art, and the landscaped garden links the original house to the Garden Wing. Contemporary pleasures include an infinity pool in the spa. If your money doesn't stretch to a room, take afternoon tea in the drawing room in front of the open fire. Life doesn't get much better. *Upper Merrion St.* ☎ *01-603 0600. www.merrionhotel.com. 143 units. Doubles €285–€450. AE, DC, MC, V. Map p 138.*

★ **Mespil Hotel** In a lovely quiet location on Grand Canal, the standard rooms in this huge hotel are bright and simple, with plain colors and crisp cotton and nothing too flashy. Many rooms have a double and single bed; good for families, or party-goers happy with a short walk home. *Mespil Rd.* ☎ *01-488 4600. www.mespilhotel.com. 255 units. Doubles €105–€205. AE, DC, MC, V. Map p 138.*

★★ **Morrison Hotel** One of Dublin's coolest designer hotels, this is swathed in soft browns, dark wood, stone floors, and creams. All rooms and lobby are simple and zen-like with a hint of the Orient from John Rocha. Relaxing colors and dimly lit corridors encourage hushed tones, with huge mirrors and tasteful artwork in the lobby. A fashionable hangout, check out the bar at weekends. *Ormond Quay.* ☎ *01-887 2400. www.morrisonhotel.ie. 138 units. Doubles €195–€340. AE, DC, MC, V. Map p 137.*

★★★ **Number 31** A romantic, luxury hideaway in converted classical Georgian coach houses, with sumptuous décor; this was architect Sam Stephenson's home. The contemporary sunken lounge sets the scene, and rooms have stylish, strong colors with brown marble bathrooms; family rooms are also available. Guests rightly rave about the breakfasts—all homemade dishes. Try and request a quiet room with a view. *31 Leeson Close.* ☎ *01-676 5011. www.number31.ie. 21 units. Doubles €150–€320. AE, DC, MC, V. Map p 138.*

★ **O'Callaghan Stephen's Green Hotel** Part of the O'Callaghan Group, which has several more hotels by Merrion Square, this is a decent mid-range option although it's worthwhile trying for a special offer. At the corner of St Stephen's Green, rooms are simple and stylish, in dark wood and some with a small terrace. Popular with business travelers, its lobby area is busy, bright, and friendly. The terrace is a little disappointing. *St Stephen's Green.* ☎ *01-607 3600. www.ocallaghanhotels.com. 78 units. Doubles €135–€335. AE, DC, MC, V. Map p 138.*

★ **Park Inn** This is part of the old Jameson's distillery in spruced-up Smithfield. Quirky touches such as glass-walled bathrooms and transparent sinks in the rooms may be style over substance, but rooms in general are fresh and contemporary, and you can't miss the huge mural of Chief O'Neil. It's worth paying a little extra for a funky suite with huge decked balcony. *Smithfield Village.* ☎ *01-817 3838. www.dublin.parkinn.ie. 73 units. Doubles €100–€230. AE, MC, V. Luas: Smithfield. Map p 137.*

★ **Parliament** This is a majestic building in the middle of the action, opposite City Hall and near Temple Bar. Recent refurbishments include double-glazing in all the front rooms to minimize street noise. Rooms are spacious, in simple dark wood and bold colors, most with double or twin beds, and family rooms are huge. The Parliament is busy and friendly and puts on a good breakfast. *Lord Edward St.* ☎ *01-670 8777. www.regencyhotels.com. 63 units. Doubles €100–€200. AE, DC, MC, V. Map p 138.*

★★ **Radisson SAS Royal** A luxury hotel opened in 2007 in the Liberties, a quiet residential area in the city center. Decent-sized rooms are elegant in slate grey and chocolate browns, with flat screen TV and free Internet, and wonderful power showers in the bathroom. Check out the huge roof terrace or, for a tad

extra, enjoy a view of St Patrick's Cathedral from a 7th-floor suite. *Golden Lane.* ☎ *01-898 2900. www.dublin.radissonsas.com. 150 units. Doubles €160–€190. AE, DC, MC, V. Map p 138.*

★ **Schoolhouse Hotel** Set in a school built in 1859, the exterior looks like a gothic church, with turrets and stone archways. Inside the small, friendly hotel, the simple bright rooms are decked out in flowery fabrics and walls, with each room named after a different Irish writer. Located a good 15 minutes walk from town, its location on the Grand Canal suits those seeking a quiet break. The bar and dining area both have high wood-beamed ceilings. *2–8 Northumberland Rd.* ☎ *01-667 5014. www.schoolhouse hotel.com. 31 units. Doubles €179–€199 w/breakfast. AE, DC, MC, V. Map p 138.*

★★ **The Shelbourne** The Irish Constitution was drafted here in 1922, and the revamped grande dame of Dublin hotels still attracts local politicians and dignitaries. Most of the original features remain, from the Waterford chandelier and marble-clad lobby (now larger), to rooms with an antique feel but modern comforts. Opulent, classy, and usually fully booked, the original rooms facing St

A touch of glam at the Shelbourne.

Stephen's Green are more traditional and high-ceilinged, the newer wing's are smaller. Take tea in the Lord Mayor's Lounge or spruce up in the Spa. *27 St Stephen's Green.* ☎ *01-663 4599. www.theshelbourne.ie. 265 units. Doubles €235–€355. AE, DC, MC, V. Map p 138.*

★ Staunton's on the Green

One of many Georgian guesthouses, this is less overpriced than most. Once a home of Henry Grattan, this overlooks St Stephen's Green and backs onto Iveagh Gardens. Refurbished rooms are modern in light wood, and the period furniture in the small lounge is welcoming, especially with the open fire. *83 St Stephen's Green South.* ☎ *01-478 2300. www. stauntonsonthegreen.ie. 57 units. Doubles €150–€165 including breakfast. AE, MC, V. Metro: Map p 138.*

★★ Trinity College

Thankfully you don't need to be scholarly to sleep here, where over the summer vacation great deals are available in historic student accommodation blocks. Favoring single and twin rooms rather than doubles, most units have two rooms sharing private bathroom, lounge, and kitchen. Breakfast vouchers are issued for the campus canteen. It's especially recommended for single travelers. *Trinity College Accommodation Office, College Green.* ☎ *01-896 1177. www.tcd.ie. 700 units. From €58 per person w/breakfast. Available mid June–late Sept. MC, V. Map p 138.*

★★ Westin

Adjacent to Trinity, the location is spot on. An Allied Irish Bank until 1998, this listed building from the 1860s retains its banking theme with original vaults now housing the basement Mint Bar. Rooms are ornate and plush, with ultra-comfy beds and WiFi throughout, but take the chance to see the fabulous glass atrium. Triple-glazed windows keep the noise out.

Lounge music at The Westbury.

College Green, Westmoreland St. ☎ *01-645 1000. www.westin.com/ dublin. 163 units. Doubles €235–€460. AE, DC, MC, V. Map p 138.*

★★ The Westbury

Grafton Street's only hotel is a longstanding favorite with upscale shoppers. Newly modernized rooms include wall-mounted plasma screen, pale silks, and handmade Irish furniture, and the lounge has a "boutique hotel" makeover. Afternoon tea in the lounge accompanied by a pianist is still an institution. *Grafton St.* ☎ *01-679 1122. www.jurysdoyle. com. 205 units. Doubles €315–€500. AE, DC, MC, V. Map p 138.*

★★ Wynn's Hotel

Near O'Connell Street, Wynn's has been around since 1845—check out the plaque in the 1st floor bar marking a meeting held by Padraig Pearse in November 1913. Rooms have a fresh look since refurbishment, with lovely dark wood furniture, writing desk, and plasma TV. Ask for a quieter room at the back or upper floors. Friendly and decent value, the family rooms are a good size. *35–39 Lower Abbey St.* ☎ *01-874 5131. www.wynnshotel.ie. 65 units. Doubles €130–€175. AE, DC, MC, V. Luas: Abbey St. Map p 137.* ●

Dún Laoghaire to Dalkey

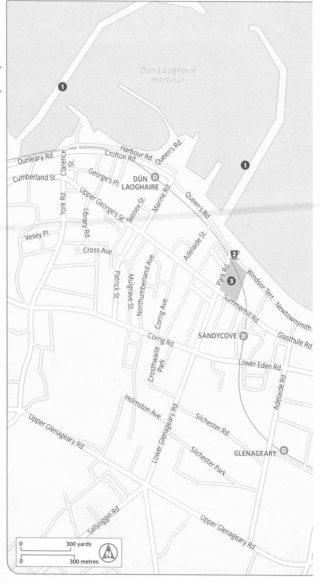

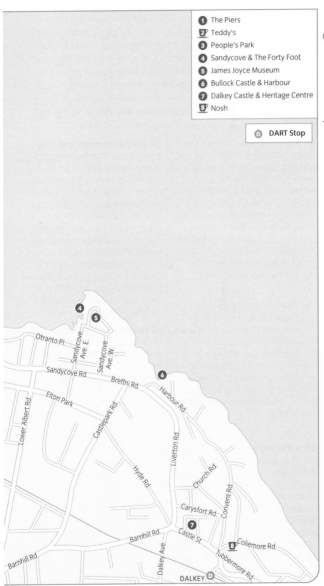

1. The Piers
2. Teddy's
3. People's Park
4. Sandycove & The Forty Foot
5. James Joyce Museum
6. Bullock Castle & Harbour
7. Dalkey Castle & Heritage Centre
8. Nosh

DART Stop

A popular day trip for locals, the port town of recently regenerated Dún Laoghaire just 11km (18 miles) south of Dublin is easily accessed by the DART light railway. From the harbor, take the coastal walk to Sandycove—the only sandy beach in the vicinity and home to the James Joyce Tower. After a spot of seal-spotting or fishing in Bullock Harbour, end the walk standing atop the Castle and Heritage Centre in stylish Dalkey, amid swanky boutiques and mansions. The hardy can continue the coastal walk to the golden beaches of Kiliney. Even if the walk is too tough for young children, Dún Laoghaire on its own makes a great day out.

❶ ★★ **The piers.** The west and east piers close to the DART station, and both popular promenading spots, jut out among the yachts, fishing boats, and huge Holyhead passenger ferry. A touch of sunshine brings everyone out onto the piers, made into decent walkways, with families, roller-bladers, joggers, and slow strollers striding out. If you return here at the end of the day, the place is likely to be packed.

❷ **Teddy's.** Going strong since 1957, Ireland's most famous ice-cream shop has them queuing down the road for the house favorite—a 99 flake (ice cream with a flakey chocolate bar). They also sell the sort of candies you haven't seen since childhood and yes, they still rot your teeth.... *1A Windsor Terrace.* ☎ *01-284 5128. $.*

❸ ★ **People's Park.** Near the town center, the People's Park comes to life on Sundays during the Farmers' Market (a relatively new concept in Dublin). Cheeses, bread, cakes, and fruit stalls lie between hot food, crafts, and gifts. Good for stocking up for a picnic or grabbing a dish of freshly made couscous (weather permitting). *Market: Sun 10am–5pm.*

Ornate fountain in People's Park.

❹ ★★ **Sandycove and The Forty Foot.** The tiny cove of golden sand is a haven for families and anyone seeking precious sun. Not surprisingly it gets packed at warm weekends. The historic Forty Foot, once a "Gentleman's bathing place" now accepts women swimmers. A chilly dip even in summer, Forty Foot is the venue of the Christmas Day swim for the truly hardy. Look for the signs indicating the seal preservation area, and what to do if one comes swimming by, which is basically "look but don't touch".

❺ **James Joyce Museum.** Easy to spot from your walk, the sturdy Martello Tower (one of many along Ireland's east coast built to withstand Napoleonic invasions) now houses the James Joyce Museum. The novelist wrote and set his opening episode of *Ulysses* here, when our hero Leopold Bloom starts out inside "a Martello Tower in Sandycove" on June 16, an ordinary day. The celebrations of the tome, known as Bloomsday, kick off every year on that day from this location. (See *Bloomsday celebrations*, p 162). The small museum now houses some of Joyce's personal possessions and rare editions of the cherished novel. The gun platform, also described in *Ulysses*, offers sweeping views of the sea. *Joyce Tower,*

Practical Matters: Dún Laoghaire

Catch the **DART** to Dún Laoghaire and Dalkey from Connolly Station, Tara Street, Pearce, and Grand Canal Dock. Single tickets cost around €2. Services run approx every 10–15 mins Mon–Sat (6.15am–midnight); every 30 mins Sun (9am–midnight). Info line ☎1850 366 222; 24-hour talking timetable: ☎ 1890 77 88 99. **Tourist Information Office** is located at the Dún Laoghaire Ferry Terminal, open Mon–Sat 10am–12.45pm and 2pm–6pm; closed Sun.

Sandycove ☎ 01-280 9265. Admission: €7 adults, €6 (concs). Mar–Oct: Mon–Sat 10am –1pm and 2–5pm, Sun & p/hols 2–6pm, Nov–Feb by arrangement only. Inc on Dublin Pass.

⑥ ★★ Bullock Castle and Harbour.

Now owned by Carmelite Sisters, the castle was once inhabited by monks who used to charge the fishermen a quota of fish they caught on the open seas. Without payment, they wouldn't be allowed back in the harbor. These days the tiny Bullock Harbour, with surprisingly tame seals bobbing up between the boats, has no such fishy taxes, not even from the two small rental stalls with 5m (16-ft) fishing boats for hire. ID is required, and those with no sailing experience will get a quick demonstration of how to use the engine. Fishing gear is also for hire, so try your hand at catching mackerel or codling. *Boat hire: 2 on Bullock Harbour (unnamed); ☎ 01-280 6517; 01-280 0915. Late May–mid Sep. €30/hr sailing; €20/hr fishing. Rods: €8/session. Daily, dawn–dusk.*

⑦ Dalkey Castle & Heritage Centre.

Fitting in pretty well with Dalkey's luxury is the Castle and Heritage Centre, comprising a 15th-century Town House, a 10th-century church and graveyard, a modern exhibition area, an art gallery, and a new writer's gallery. Introductory tours of the castle include a Living History Experience, with costumed medieval archers giving a lively historical flavor and background to the language. *Castle St, Dalkey. ☎ 01-285 8366. www.dalkeycastle. com. €6 adults, concs €5, children €4. Mon–Fri 9.30am–5pm; Sat, Sun & p/hols 11am–5pm. Costumed guides May–Oct.*

⑧ Nosh.

A super place to end the day, whether with a Bloody Mary, Barbary duck, or good old fish and chips. Small, cozy, and very popular and of course oozing Dalkey style. *111 Coliemore Road, Dalkey. ☎ 01-284 0666. $$.*

Busy Dún Laoghaire pier.

Malahide

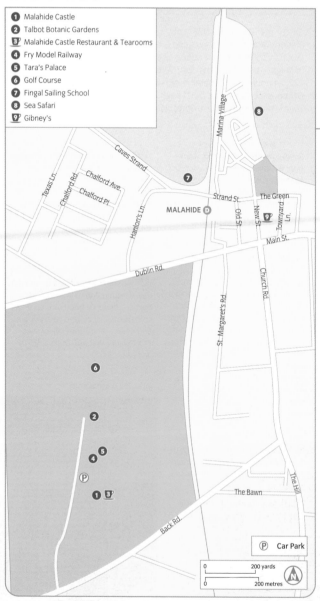

1 Malahide Castle
2 Talbot Botanic Gardens
3 Malahide Castle Restaurant & Tearooms
4 Fry Model Railway
5 Tara's Palace
6 Golf Course
7 Fingal Sailing School
8 Sea Safari
9 Gibney's

Caves Strand

Texas Ln.
Chalford Rd.
Chalford Ave.
Chalford Pl.
Hanlon's Ln.

Marina Village

Strand St.
Old St.
New St.
The Green
Townyard Ln.

MALAHIDE

Main St.

Dublin Rd.

St. Margaret's Rd.

Church Rd.

The Bawn

The Hill

Back Rd.

P Car Park

0   200 yards
0   200 metres

The pretty seaside town of Malahide, 13km (8 miles) north of Dublin, is a day out that covers a pretty broad base of interests. Centered around the huge castle, the grounds of which are superb and now the venue for huge concerts, there are two gorgeous little museums—tailor-made for kids—plus botanic gardens. Its nearby municipal-run golf course provides probably the cheapest 9-hole round in Ireland. The coast offers watersports and a sea safari, and even a bird sanctuary around Broadmeadow Estuary. During the summer, the castle and grounds may be closed due to weekend concerts. Many of the other attractions are closed throughout winter.

1 ★★ Malahide Castle. Set among 102 hectares (250 acres) of parkland, the castle was a fortress and, since 1185, a private home to the Talbot family, the last of whom died in 1973. They even managed to keep hold of it after Cromwell's march through Ireland. A perfectly preserved period house, the furnishings, portraits, and family tragedies come to life during the tour: the excellent audio guide includes the moving tale of the morning of the Battle of the Boyne in 1690, when 14 members of the family took breakfast in the drawing room and all were killed that day. The furnishings are exquisite, including 18th-century gilt tables, heavy fabrics, and carved-oak walls. Keep a look out for one of five ghosts said to parade the abode, including the Talbot's 16th-century jester, Puck.

Malahide Castle's tower.

Tours around the house are by group only. *Malahide.* ☎ *01-846 2184. Admission: €7 adults, €6 seniors & students, €4 children. Daily 10am–12.45pm and 2–5pm; April–Sept: Mon—at 10am–5pm; Sun and hols 10am–6pm. Groups leave every 15–30 mins.*

2 ★★ Talbot Botanic Gardens. The walled garden, accessed via the back of the house, seems to be forgotten by most visitors, so make the most of its tranquility. Created by Lord Milo Talbot between 1948 and 1973, it covers more than 8 hectares (nearly 20 acres) of shrubbery and 1.5 hectares (3.7 acres) of walled garden. Lord Milo apparently had a soft spot for southern hemisphere plants, but even if you don't know your clematis from your berberis, it's still great for a peaceful stroll. Open only during summer. *Malahide Castle,* ☎ *01-846 2456. Admission: €4.50 adults, seniors and under 12 free. May–Sept: Daily 2–5pm. Guided tour Weds 2pm.*

3 kids Malahide Castle Restaurant & Tearooms. Even if you haven't done the castle tour, the restaurant and tearooms within the house are a good pit-stop in historic surroundings for scones, soup, sandwiches, or even a decent three-course lunch, though it can get busy at weekends. *Malahide Castle,* ☎ *01-846 3027. $.*

The Best Day Trips & Excursions

Lush flora at Talbot Botanic Gardens.

④ ★★★ Fry Model Railway. You don't have to be a trainspotter to find this miniature working railway utterly charming. A narrator brings the history of the railways to life, and spotlights lead you round the huge 232-square meter (2,500-square foot) model of Dublin. Complete with Georgian houses, riverbanks, and farms, the tracks cover 600m (2000 ft) and circumnavigate the entire scene. The handmade models of Irish trains were completed with incredible attention to detail by rail enthusiast Cyril Fry between the 1930s and the 1960s. Even his wife Mary spent years painting and casting the tiny trains. Tracks and models range from the earliest Irish locomotives and the Guinness steam barge, right up to

the modern-day DART. A major treat for 3-year-olds, this one is not just for the kids. Open only during summer; access to the working model is by group only. *Malahide Castle Demesne,* ☎ *01-846 3779. Admission: €7 adults, €6 seniors & students, €4 children. Apr–Sept: Mon–Sat 10am–1pm and 2–5pm. Sun and hols 2–6pm.*

⑤ ★ Tara's Palace. Opposite the Fry Model Railway, in the grounds of the castle, this doll's house museum is a big hit with small kids and an amazing piece of work. Inspired by Titania's Palace of 1907, and built by an adoring father in response to daughter Gwendoline's dreams of fairies, this too was handmade—all 22 rooms of it. A perfect replica of the original, now in Denmark, each room is filled with meticulously detailed handmade furniture including a four-poster bed, rocking horses, and paintings. This is the centerpiece to other exhibits, all made by Irish craftsmen. Look out for Portobello, circa 1700, a doll's house that belonged to Oscar Wilde's mother. *Malahide Castle Demesne,* ☎ *01-846 2779. Admission: €3 adults, under 5 free. Apr–Sept: Mon–Sat 10am–1pm and 2–5pm. Sun and p/hols 2–6pm.*

Find your dream home in Tara's Palace.

Practical Matters: Malahide

Catch the **DART** to Malahide from city center stations including Connolly Station, Tara Street, Pearce, and Grand Canal Dock. Single tickets cost around €2. Services run approx every 10–15 mins Mon–Sat (6.15am–midnight); every 30 mins Sun (9am–midnight). The **Nitelink** night bus 42N goes half-hourly from Malahide to Dublin center.

6 ★★ **Golf course.** Although not for the likes of Tiger Woods, recreational golfers, beginners, and children will love these 2 municipal-run courses, comprising an 18-hole (short) pitch-and-putt, and 9-hole par-3 courses. What's the attraction? Anyone can turn up and play a round at an absurdly low cost, even for hiring the clubs. Located in the grounds of the castle, near the Dublin Road entrance, the space is beautiful and well maintained. *Malahide Castle Demesne,* ☎ *01-846 2779. Admission: €3 adults, under 5 free. Apr–Sept: Mon–Sat 10am–1pm and 2–5pm. Sun and hols 2–6pm.*

7 ★ **Fingal Sailing School.** Located by the Marina, the sailing school offers short courses in surfing, kayaking, and sailing, but equipment can also be rented for a quick blast on the water. Anyone renting must have basic proficiency and a level 1 sailing certificate. Wetsuits and buoyancy aids are all provided, just bring your taste for the outdoors. The school is open year-round, although rentals are available only between June and early September. *Upper Strand, Malahide,* ☎ *01-845 1979. Daily 9am–5pm, sometimes later in summer.*

8 ★ **Sea Safari.** For the adventurous, and children over 8, this safari taking 1¼ hours gets you up close to the island known as Ireland's Eye, a visit to a cave, and around Howth Harbour: great for spotting cormorants and puffins, and the odd seal. The speedy motorized RIB (rigid inflatable boat) bounces along the water in good weather only, between March and October. Bring something to keep your camera dry. *Malahide Marina,* ☎ *01-806 1626. Trips run approximately every hour; no fixed times. Advanced booking advisable.*

9 **Gibney's.** In the middle of the pretty town, and going strong since 1937, Gibney's is a fine choice to end the day with decent bar food, good beers and wines, and plenty of lively locals. Split into several areas, including a wonderful beer garden, it hosts nightly entertainment including music and comedy. *New Street, Malahide,* ☎ *01-845 0606. $.*

Malahide's peaceful marina.

Howth

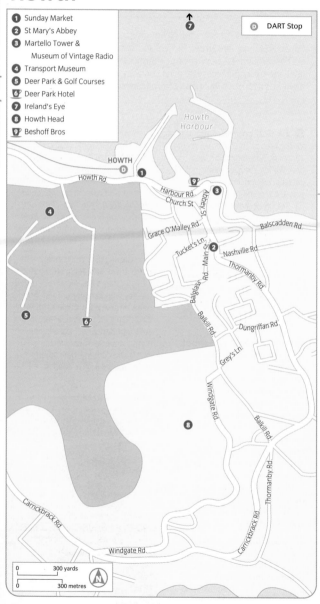

1. Sunday Market
2. St Mary's Abbey
3. Martello Tower &
   Museum of Vintage Radio
4. Transport Museum
5. Deer Park & Golf Courses
6. Deer Park Hotel
7. Ireland's Eye
8. Howth Head
9. Beshoff Bros

D DART Stop

Howth Harbour

HOWTH

Howth Rd.

Harbour Rd.
Church St
Abbey St.
Grace O'Malley Rd.
Balscadden Rd.
Tucket's Ln.
Nashville Rd.
Main St.
Thormanby Rd.
Balglass Rd.
Balkill Rd.
Dungriffan Rd.
Grey's Ln.
Windgate Rd.
Balkill Rd.
Thormanby Rd.
Carrickbrack Rd.
Carrickbrack Rd.
Windgate Rd.

0   300 yards
0   300 metres

Relaxing Howth has its splash of luxury courtesy of the yacht marina but it is better known for its wonderful coastal walks, trips to the tiny Ireland's Eye, seafood to die for, a museum containing fire engines dating back to 1860, and a busy Sunday market. Located just 10km (6 miles) north of Dublin on the scenic Howth Peninsular, this was once an island and, like most Dublin coastal towns, is easily accessible by the DART. It is possible to combine a daytrip to nearby Malahide (see p 152) but each really merits a full day, and more so for those who love walking. A touch of history comes courtesy of the Museum of Vintage Radio at Martello Tower, and sporting pleasure from the golf courses. And, as the east coast's largest fishing center, it's a great place to sample the local catch. From a sleepy fishing community to today's popular suburb, with Dubliners making the daily commute to the city, this is a great place to bring children. In fact, I enjoy Howth as much now as I did as a kid.

❶ ★ Sunday Market. Located near the West Pier, next to the DART station, the busy Sunday market's outdoor stalls are perfect for stocking up on food for the day, or simply jars of homemade pickles and preserves for gifts. It's strange to think that markets such as these have only been going since 2005. The indoor section of the market, housed along the West Pier, has rails of clothes and some unusual silver jewelry. *West Pier, Sundays 9am–5pm.*

A taste of Ireland at the Sunday Market.

❷ ★★ St Mary's Abbey. Take the steep uphill walk from the East Pier to St Mary's Abbey and grave-yard, dating back to 1042. If nothing else, the view of the waterfront from here is superb. Dedicated to the Virgin Mary, this was a collegiate, indicating it was served by a college or community of clerics who lived south of the church. It was first built in 1042 by King Sitric of Dublin, replaced in 1235, again in the second half of the 14th century, and later modified.

❸ ★★ Martello Tower & Museum of Vintage Radio. This recently restored Martello Tower is one of 34 dotted along the east coast to ward off pesky Napoleonic invasions. It hosts the quaintly named Ye Olde Hurdy Gurdy Museum of Vintage Radio, a personal collection of the delightful Pat Herbert, who is happy to show visitors the old radios, music boxes, gramophones, etc. It's fitting that the two-level museum should be here, because in 1852 one of the world's first cables was laid at this point. It was used by the American Lee de Forrest in 1903 for telegraphy experiments, and in 1905 the Marconi Company conducted ship-to-shore

A stunning view of St Mary's Abbey.

wireless experiments from here. On Sunday mornings, you'll probably see amateur radio station EI0MAR operating at the tower in Morse code. *Martello Tower.* ☎ *086-815 4189. Admission: €5 adults, €3 seniors, children free (must be accompanied by adult). May–Oct daily, 11am–4pm.*

④ ★★ Transport Museum.

This collection has vehicles dating between 1883 and 1984 although it's hard to get around and it seems rather like squeezing around vehicles in a crowded car park. With the Hill of Howth tram, the Merryweather steam fire engine, and baker's vans galore, the huge horde has examples from passenger, emergency, commercial, and military vehicles. One of the most interesting is the illuminated tram, Dublin's only one, which toured the city at night advertizing parish fetes, and was badly burnt in the 1930s. Ask museum staff to point out the Merryweather fire-fighter from 1883 (the museum's oldest) and the 1889 Merryweather steam pump. Look out also for the Leyland Tiger bus from the 1930s, nicknamed in irony as "our very own Celtic Tiger". Run by volunteers, limited funding means that its 180 exhibits are crammed into a tiny space, something that may hopefully change in the next couple of years. *Heritage Depot, Howth Demesne,* ☎ *01-832 0427; 086-828 9437. Admission: €3 adults, €1.50,*

Old-time baker's van at the Transport Museum.

Local resident.

€8, Jun–Aug, Mon–Fri 10am–5pm; Sat, Sun & hols 2-5pm; Sept–May Sat, Sun 7 hols 2–5pm.

⑤ ★★ Deer Park & Golf Courses. The walk from the Transport Museum takes you through the tranquil Deer Park (although I've never spotted deer here) past Howth Castle, dating back to 1450. The castle itself has now been converted into upmarket residences and is not open for public viewing. The Rhododendron Gardens, one of Europe's largest, lie a little farther inside the park, and visitors coming in May and early June will catch the glorious blooms in reds, pinks, and purples from 40 varieties. Inside the park are the golf courses run by the Deer Park Hotel. Visitors can take their pick of very reasonably priced green fees and club hire for the pitch and putt, 9-, and 18-hole courses. *Deer Park Hotel, Deer Park, ☎ 01-832 2624; 01-832 3489. Golf courses daily 7am–7pm; winter 8am–2pm.*

Practical Matters: Howth

Catch the **DART** to Howth from city center stations including Connelly Station, Tara Street, Pearce, and Grand Canal Dock. Single tickets cost around €2. Services run approx every 10-15 mins Mon–Sat (6.15am–midnight); every 30 mins Sun (9am–midnight). Buses 31 and 31B travel to and from the city center, including Connelly Station. **Hotel:** Deer Park Hotel offers good rates, and a peaceful, scenic setting. ☎ 01-832 2624; www.deerpark-hotel.ie. **Restaurants:** An excellent fish restaurant is Aqua, West Pier, ☎ 01-832 0690. www.aqua.ie. **Nitelink** 31N night bus travels from Howth to Dublin city center every 30 mins.

6 **Deer Park Hotel.** The terrace of the hotel makes for a good stop for tea and scones, while gazing out over the greens. *Deer Park,* ☎ *01-832 2624. $.*

7 ★★ **Ireland's Eye.** Boats leave regularly during the summer for the tiny island just 2km (1.2 miles) from Howth Harbour. This rocky outcrop is perfect for the keen ornithologist, and lovers of desolate beaches, dramatic cliffs, and ruined churches. It houses a Martello Tower built in the early 19th century, and remains of a 6th-century monastic church, part of Howth's long Christian history. It is believed that the Garland of Howth, a Latin manuscript of the New Testament, now in Trinity College Library, was written here. Get out the binoculars to spot puffins, kittywakes, and cormorants, and of course seals. Tread carefully (so you don't stand on eggs) and wander the island; it's hard to believe it's so close to the city! *Boats run from East Pier,* ☎ *086-845 9154. 10am–6pm daily; evening in Jun & Jul. No fixed*

Fishing boats in Howth harbour.

Howth lighthouse.

timings, approx every 30 mins. €15 adults, €10 children.

8 ★★ **Howth Head.** If weather permits (it's no fun if it's too cloudy to see the view), take a walk along the coastline of the Howth Peninsular, passing the rugged landscape. Its summit is the perfect point to see the peninsula, with the Dublin Mountains in the background. There is a well-marked path and large map at East Pier, or take the cliffside walk. All paths are well trodden, so take whichever one you fancy. I love taking a picnic to the Howth Head for a dining experience with a spectacular view.

9 **Beshoff Bros.** Fish rarely tastes this good. Queue up for fish and chips (try the smoked haddock) with tubs of garlic sauce then savor, sitting on the pier in the setting sun: Inexpensive and wonderful. *Harbour Road,* ☎ *01-832 1754. $.* ●

The
Savvy Traveler

Before You Go

Government Tourist Offices

In the US: 345 Park Ave, 17th Floor, New York, NY 10154 (☎ 212-418-0800). Toll-free Infoline ☎ 800-22-6470. **In Canada:** (☎ 800-223-6470). **In the UK:** 103 Wigmore St, London W1U 1QS (☎ 020-518 0800). Freephone infoline (☎ 0800-039 7000). **In Australia:** ☎ 02-9299 6177.

The Best Times to Go

June to September is the best and busiest time to visit, jam-packed with festivals throughout the summer, although as a city break Dublin is popular year round. Hotels are often a little cheaper from **November to February**. There's no particular month to avoid, although be prepared for huge crowds in **March** for the St Patrick's Day celebrations, a public holiday. The **Christmas** season sees shopping areas packed in the build-up, with special markets opening. It's also a popular destination for **New Year's Eve**, especially to hear the midnight bells peal from Christ Church Cathedral, and see the New Year's Day parade.

As Ireland's capital and a base to explore the country, Dublin enjoys year-round tourism plus major sporting events, so mid- to high-range hotels should be booked well in advance.

Festivals & Special Events

SPRING. One of the highlights of the year is **St Patrick's Day** (March 17), a packed, week-long party throughout the city with a huge parade, music, fairs, and lasers, when every visitor seems to boast Irish roots—however remote. Book your hotel early for this one. ☎ 01-676 3205. www.stpatricksfestival.ie.

Temple Bar plays host to **Handel's Messiah Festival**, a week-long series of recitals and workshops celebrating the anniversary of the world premiere of this musical masterpiece, held in Dublin in 1742. ☎ 01-677 2255. www.templebar.ie.

April's **Dublin Dance Festival** has contemporary dance from around the world, with top choreographers, masterclasses, and seminars. ☎ 01-679 0524. www.dancefestivalireland.ie. In May the two-week long **Dublin Gay Theatre Festival** showcases gay contributors to Irish drama. www.gaytheatre.ie.

Summer is beckoned in with floral delights in Phoenix Park for **Bloom** (early June), with garden designs and flower shows. ☎ 01-668 5155. www.bloominthepark.com.

Tall ships, markets, and music show off the ever-changing waterfront at the **Docklands Maritime Festival** (early June). www.dublindocklands.ie.

SUMMER. **Temple Bar Diversions Festival** is a summer-long festival with outdoor film screenings in the main square, opera, and street theater. ☎ 01-677 2255. www.templebar.ie.

The week-long **Dublin Writers Festival** (mid June) gives you a chance to meet international authors and journalists to discuss their work, in various venues. ☎ 01-222 7848. www.dublinwritersfestival.com.

James Joyce fans get all Edwardian for **Bloomsday** (June 16), re-enacting or listening to his masterpiece *Ulysses* set around Dublin on this day. ☎ 01-878 8547. www.jamesjoyce.ie.

Dublin Pride enjoys two weeks of social and cultural events in June, marking the anniversary of New York's Stonewall Riots, culminating in a huge parade. www.dublinpride.org. The relatively new but well-respected

Useful Websites

www.visitdublin.com: Dublin Tourist Office's official site, with maps, sightseeing, accommodation offers, and local transport.

www.discoverireland.com: Official site of Tourism Ireland, with information on the entire country, and details on airlines flying from the US.

www.dublinks.com: Decent guide to events, sightseeing, and nightlife.

www.ireland.com: Online version of the excellent *Irish Times* newspaper, including an Ancestors section.

www.eventguide.ie: Online version of the free fortnightly What's On listing paper.

www.thedubliner.ie: Food and drink reviews, current affairs, and local arts scene.

www.dublinbus.ie: Dublin Bus, with timetables and ticket info.

www.irishrail.ie: Rail information to get around Ireland, plus DART timetables.

www.tickets.ie: Booking site for tickets for major events, with collection points around the city.

www.118.ie: Directory including shops, offices, and services from acupuncture to zip fasteners.

Oxegen music festival (July) takes over Punchestown Racecourse in Kildare for a weekend, with a heavyweight line-up of top rock and indie bands. *www.oxegen.ie.*

The city gets equine for the **Dublin Horse Show** (August) with five days of top international showjumping, including the Aga Khan Cup. ☎ *01-240 7213. www.dublinhorse show.com.* Dún Laoghaire hosts the wonderful **Festival of World Culture** weekend (late August), acknowledging Ireland's multi-ethnic population with musicians from nearly 100 countries around the world, quite possibly from Algeria to Zambia. ☎ *01-271 9555. www. festivalofworldcultures.com.*

FALL. The two-week long **Dublin Fringe Festival** (September) has a packed program of international fringe companies in various venues around town, with cabaret, music, and theater. ☎ *1850-374 643. www. fringefest.com.*

Croke Park gets busy at weekends for the **Hurling and Gaelic Football Finals** (September), when the national tournaments reach a climax. Hotel prices leap up on these dates. ☎ *01-865 8657. www. gaa.ie.*

The **Dublin Theatre Festival** (September–October) is Europe's longest-running theater festival, going strong for more than half a century, and brings a decent selection of international theater, plus new Irish plays, to various venues. ☎ *01-677 8439. www.dublintheatre festival.com.* Ghouls, ghosts, and costumed street artists come out to play for the **Samhain Hallowe'en Parade** (October 31) through the city center, originally a pagan festival celebrating the dead and start of winter. Be prepared for fireworks and—of course—much drinking.

WINTER. Christmas does have its spiritual side after all, with traditional Mass and candlelit services at the **Christmas Eve Vigil at St Mary's Pro-Cathedral**, with music from the famous Palestrina Choir. Then get earthy and blow your Christmas money at the **Christmas Racing Festival** (December 26) at Leopardstown, the start of a four-day festival at one of Ireland's premier racecourses. ☎ *01-289 0500. www.leopardstown.com.*

Ring in the New Year with **Christ Church Bells** at midnight, where locals gather to hear Ireland's loudest peals. ☎ *01-677 8099. www. cccdub.ie.* Traditional Irish music and culture comes alive at **Temple Bar Trad** (February), where you see jigs and reels performed by great musicians in cozy bars and cultural venues. ☎ *01-677 2397. www.temple bartrad.com.*

The Weather
With a cool, damp climate pretty much year-round, don't come to Dublin for a suntan. The warmest months are June to August, when there could be the odd hot spell, and most hotels will have air-conditioning, if not a fan.

It's always important to remember that it can rain at any time; be prepared for it, bring waterproofs, and take on the local cheerful attitude towards the odd shower, treating a sunny day and clear skies as a bonus. After all, this is what makes Ireland as green as it is.

The nights draw in, and winter sets in, from November to February, although the temperature rarely reaches freezing.

Cellphones
Cellphones in the US may be different from those in Ireland. If you are planning on traveling abroad, it may be easier to ensure your phone has GSM technology; most tri-band phones will work over in Ireland and some dual-band (1800MHz) may work also. Check with your phone manufacturer. Contact your cell-phone server to ensure you have roaming facility. Rent a handset through **Cell-phone-Ireland.com**, or through **rentaphone-ireland. com**, which you can order from the US (☎ 353-876-834-563) and nominate a pick-up point in Ireland. It may be better value to buy a new handset (with plenty of low-cost options) from **Carphone Warehouse** 30 Grafton St, (☎ 01-670 5265); or 2 Henry St (☎ 01-878 470). If your phone is compatible with other sim cards, it works out much cheaper to buy a local sim (networks include O2, Vodafone, Meteor, and 3) to make local calls, as phoning or receiving calls from your overseas number may be prohibitively expensive.

Car Rentals
Driving within Dublin is neither advised nor necessary, given the expensive parking, dreadful traffic jams, relatively cheap taxis, and decent bus service. Should you wish to drive farther afield, for example to explore Kildare, Wicklow, or Hill of Tara, it's better to book ahead via Avis, Budget, Hertz, and the like. Most convenient is to book via the Dublin Tourism website (www.visit dublin.com); their section "Getting Around" includes car hire, with all the companies displayed on one page making a price comparison easy.

Getting **There**

By Plane
Dublin Airport, with a much-needed second terminal opening in 2009, is the base of budget airline Ryanair, with cheap flights to and from Europe. Long-haul airlines flying to Dublin include Aer Lingus (the national airline), Delta Air Lines, American Airlines, Continental, Air Canada, and British Airways. There is a far greater selection of routes that would involve changing in London, UK.

From the airport (10km (6.5 miles) north of the city center) there are several ways to get into town, all of which leave from outside the arrivals hall. The double-decker **Airlink** (adults €6/children €3) has 2 similar services: No 747 travels via O'Connell Street to Central Bus Station (Busaras) every 10 minutes 5.30am–11pm, taking around 35 minutes. No 748 also goes via Central Bus Station but ends up at Heuston Railway Station, taking around 45 minutes. The single-decker **Aircoach** (adults €7/children €1) goes to Ballsbridge via O'Connell Street, Grafton Street, and Merrion Square every 10 minutes 6am–8pm, every 20 minutes 8pm–midnight and every hour through the night. It takes around 45 minutes to reach Grafton St. Slowest and cheapest is the public bus, **Dublin Bus** (€2), making frequent stops into town and taking around an hour. **Taxis** wait outside the arrivals hall, with a metered fare into town around €25–30, although it's slower and more expensive in rush hour.

It is important to allow plenty of time when traveling **to** the airport, as traffic is very slow especially during the after-work rush hour, and on weekends when there is a major match at Croke Park.

By Car
The **N11** highway leads to Dublin from Dún Laoghaire harbor (and car ferry), the **N1** and **M1** from Belfast in the north, the **N6 and N4** from Galway in the west, and the **N8** and **N7** from Cork in the south. Signs to **City Centre** (*An Lar*) will clearly be posted as you approach Dublin. From the airport, take the **M1**.

By Train
There are two railway stations in Dublin run by **Irish Rail** (www.irishrail.ie): **Connolly Station** (☎ 01-703 2358) has services to Belfast and Sligo; trains from **Heuston Station** (☎ 01-703 3299) include Cork, Tralee, Limerick, Waterford, Galway, and Kildare. The InterRail Global Pass and InterRail One Country Pass are both valid throughout Ireland. (www.interrailnet.com).

By Ferry
Despite the plethora of cheap flights to Ireland, plenty of car-ferries still operate the Dublin route from the UK. **Irish Ferries** (☎ 0818-300 400; www.irishferries.com) run speedy car ferries between **Dublin** and **Holyhead** (North Wales) several times a day, plus **Rosslare** to **Pembroke**. **Norfolkline** (☎ UK: 0870-600 4321; Ireland: 01-819 2999; www.norfolkline-ferries.co.uk) have day and night crossings between **Liverpool** and **Dublin** taking around seven hours. **Stena Line** (☎ UK: 08705-204 204; Ireland: 01-204 7777; www.stenaline.co.uk) runs separate services from **Holyhead** to both **Dún Laoghaire** and **Dublin Port**. **P&O Irish Sea** (☎ UK: 08705-980 333) have two ferries daily between **Liverpool** and **Dublin**.

Getting **Around**

By Bus
Sorely missing an underground system, **Dublin Bus** (☎ 01-873 4222; www.dublinbus.ie) network covers most of the city, although it can be overworked and slow-going in rush hour. Pay by exact change only to the driver (always worth having a bundle of coins handy) with fares depending on what stage you board. Most city center journeys cost between €1 and €2. If you're doing several journeys, it's worth getting a 1-day (€6) or 3-day (€11) ticket, valid on the Airlink bus, allowing unlimited bus journeys. Timetables and routes are usually displayed at the bus stops. **Nitelink** buses run from 11.30pm Monday to Saturday from the city center to the suburbs; flat fare €4.

By Luas
The **Luas** new light rail system (☎ 01-461 4910; www.luas.ie) is wonderfully comfortable, good value, and frequent. It's just a shame that the only two lines in the city don't actually meet up. The Green Line runs along the southeast of the city, from St Stephen's Green to Sandyford, via Dundrum. The Red Line starts at Connolly Station running along the north bank of the Liffey through Four Courts and Smithfield to Heuston Station, then down the southwest suburbs to Tallaght. Single and return tickets are bought from the machines on the platform (change given); daily passes are also available.

By DART
The Dublin Area Rapid Transport or **DART** operates speedy, green trains at great value to coastal areas out of town. The nearest city center stations are Pearse (south of the Liffey) and Connolly (north), taking around 20 minutes to Dún Laoghaire (€2), even less to Howth and Malahide. Get tickets from the machines or counter at the station, or buy a one-day pass, which works out cheaper if making more than two longer journeys.

By Taxi
Taxis are plentiful and relatively cheap in Dublin, just flag one down on the street. There are private hire cab offices all around the city; every hotel, restaurant, bar, and club will probably have the number of their local one. Evening taxi ranks include Dame St opposite College Green, and another near City Hall, Dawson Street opposite Mansion House, Merrion Row near St Stephen's Green, and St Andrew Street outside the post office. All taxis are on the meter, starting at €3.80 (€4.10 8pm–8am and Sundays) with an extra €2 if booked in advance.

On Foot
Dublin is the perfect walking city, with many of the places of interest in a small, compact center. It is also a city where the getting from A to B is half the fun, discovering unexpected delights along the way. Bring comfortable walking shoes, be prepared for showers, and try and do as much as you can on foot.

Fast **Facts**

Apartment Rentals   Gulliver Ireland (☎ 066-979 2030; www.gulliver.ie) is a good agency for renting apartments and holiday homes in the Dublin area; the **Dublin Tourism** website has deals for self-catering accommodations (www.visitdublin.com); The official **Tourism Ireland** website (www.discoverireland.com) lists serviced apartments and townhouses, including in the city center.

ATMs/Cashpoints   Most banks have 24-hour ATMs, which accept Maestro, Cirrus, and Visa cards, and are found especially in the main shopping areas. Exchange currency either at banks or travel agents like Thomas Cook; check the rates of all exchange offices as rates and commission differs. Usually your bank back home will charge you for withdrawing money overseas. Major Irish banks include Bank of Ireland, Allied Irish Bank, and Ulster Bank. (See also Money.)

Business Hours   Banks are open Monday–Friday, 10am–4pm, with most open till 5pm on Thursday. Most offices are open Monday–Friday 10am–5pm. At restaurants, lunch is usually 12–3pm and dinner 7–10.30pm. Major stores are open Monday–Saturday 9.30/10am–6pm; late-night shopping on Thursday till 8pm; Sundays from 11–4/5pm, although not all stores are open on Sundays. Many museums close one day a week, mostly on Mondays, including the National Museums.

Consulates and Embassies   US Embassy, 42 Elgin Rd, Ballsbridge (☎ 01-668 8777); **Canadian Embassy,** 7–8 Wilton Terrace, (☎ 01-417 4100); **British Embassy,** 29 Merrion Rd, Ballsbridge (☎ 01-205 3700); **Australian Embassy,**

7th Floor, Fitzwilton House, Wilton Terrace (☎ 01-664 5300).

Credit Cards   Call your credit card company the minute you discover your credit card has been lost or stolen, and file a report at the nearest police station (Garda). Bring the telephone number from back home to report the theft and cancel the card. To report loss or theft of **American Express** cards from Ireland, US residents should call Global Assist on 001-715-343-7977; UK residents call 1850-882-028. To report a stolen **Visa** Card, call 1800-55 8802. Your pin number is required when using your credit card at all outlets.

Doctors   Ask at your hotel for a local doctor.

Electricity   Most hotels operate on 230 volts AC (50 cycles), three-pin plugs. Adaptors can be provided at major hotels.

Emergencies   Dial ☎ 999 for police, ambulance, or fire emergencies. (See also *Insurance* p 168.)

Gay & Lesbian Travelers   Dublin's city center might not be on a par with New York's Greenwich Village or London's Soho for gay lifestyle, but it's pretty good and relatively liberal, compared with the suburbs. Although there are very few gay bars and clubs, many venues have gay nights, which attract a mixed friendly crowd. The gay-friendly social scene has grown and improved over recent years, although outward displays of same-sex affection aren't particularly the done thing. **Gay Community News** (www.gcn.ie) is a great guide to what's on in the city. The **International Dublin Gay Theatre Festival** was established to commemorate the 150th anniversary of the birth of Oscar Wilde, Dublin's most celebrated gay man.

Holidays Public holidays: January 1 (New Year's Day), March 17 (St Patrick's Day), March/April (Good Friday and Easter Monday), 1st Mon in May (May Day), 1st Mon in June (June Bank Holiday), 1st Mon in August (August Bank Holiday), last Mon in October (Hallowe'en), 25 December (Christmas Day), 26 December (St Stephen's Day).

Insurance Check your existing insurance policies before you buy travel insurance to cover trip cancellation, lost luggage, medical expenses, or car rental insurance. Recommended insurers include: **Access America** (☎ 800-284-8300; www.accessamerica.com); **Travel Assistance International** (☎ 800-821-2828; www.travel assistance.com); and for medical insurance **MEDEX Assistance** (☎ 800-732-5309; www.medex assist.com). UK citizens should take an **EHIC** card (the old E-111), for free or heavily discounted emergency medical treatment within the EU. ID should also be brought if requiring emergency medical treatment.

Internet Internet access is plenti-ful: in cybercafés, small convenience stores, and basic places above shops also offering cheap interna-tional calls, and many also have Skype facilities. Most hotels now offer WiFi or broadband in their rooms. In the near future, the **Temple Bar** area may all be WiFi connected.

Lost Property If your luggage gets lost in transit from a flight, reg-ister this with your airline at the air-port. For all thefts, report to a local police station (Garda). For loss or theft of credit cards, see *Credit Cards* above. Other useful numbers: **Bus Eireann** (Central Bus Station) ☎ 01-836 6111; **Heuston Station** ☎ 01-703 2102; **Connolly Station** ☎ 01-703 2362; **Taxis lost prop-erty** ☎ 01-666 9850.

Mail and Postage Mail boxes are green, post offices are called An Post. Most famous of all is the **General Post Office**, O'Connell St ☎ 01-705 7000, opening hours Mon–Sat 8am–8pm. For **Poste Restante** collection, bring photo ID. Other city center post offices include: 16 Merrion Row, ☎ 01 -676 5961 and 1A Earlsfort Terrace, ☎ 01-662 3192. Opening hours for both are Monday–Friday 9am–1pm and 2.15–5.30pm; Saturday 9am–1pm. A letter or postcard sent within Ireland costs €0.55; to US, UK, and rest of the world €0.78.

Money The single European cur-rency in Ireland is the **euro**, which is used in 15 other European countries (but not the UK). At press time, the exchange rate was approximately €1 = \$1.44 (or £0.70). For up-to-the minute exchange rates, check the currency converter website **www.xe.com**. Euros are available at all ATMs and exchange booths. The main Tourist Office on Suffolk St has a Fexco Bureau de Change.

Passports No visas are required for US, UK, Canadian, Australian, or New Zealand visitors to Ireland, for stays of up to 90 days. If your passport is lost or stolen, contact your country's embassy or consulate immediately (see *Con-sulates & Embassies* p 167). Make a copy of your passport's critical pages before you leave and keep it separate from your passport.

Pharmacies Pharmacies operate during normal business hours, with a green cross clearly displayed out-side, and some open till 10pm in the city center. There are no all-night pharmacies. **City Pharmacy** (14 Dame St, ☎ 01-670 4523) is open every day until 10pm. **Boots the**

Chemist (20 Henry St, ☎ 01-873 0209; Unit 113, St Stephen's Green, ☎ 01-478 4368; 12 Grafton St., ☎ 01-677 3000) is open until 9pm most nights except Sunday.

Police The national police (Garda) emergency number is ☎ 999 or 112. Local police stations in the city include **Pearse Street** (☎ 01-666 9000); **Store Street** (☎ 01-666 8000); **Harcourt Terrace** (☎ 01-666 9500).

Safety Take the usual precautions in major cities, such as watch your bags and valuables in busy places, avoid walking in dark quiet areas alone at night, including Phoenix Park, take your money away quickly from the ATM and keep your pin well hidden, and keep money out of your back pocket. Most crime is drink or drug-related, with drunken revellers a common sight in the city center at weekends. If in doubt, avoid crowds like these. Drug dealers have been known to hang around the Liffey Boardwalk; look confident and don't make eye contact.

Smoking Smoking has been banned in all public transport and other public places, since 2004. The locals seem to have adapted well to the smoking ban in pubs, clubs, and restaurants, and a noticeable change is the improvement to outside spaces and terraces.

Taxes Value-added tax (VAT) is 21% on most goods, excluding food, books, and children's clothes. Most hotels include tax when quoting the price. Non-EU residents are entitled to a reimbursement of VAT, at shops with the **Global Refund Tax Free Shopping** sign displayed. Ask the shop assistant for the Global Refund Cheque (there is no minimum spend for this), get it stamped, and take it to your last port of call when leaving the EU (in this case usually Dublin Airport). Get your cash (or credit card) refund at the Global Refund

office at the airport before you fly. For more information see www. globalrefund.com.

Telephones For national directory enquiries, ☎ 11850; for international ☎ 114. There are telephone boxes dotted around the city, either coin operated or with pre-paid phonecards (available from newsagents and post offices). The code for Dublin is 01, not required if you are calling from Dublin except from a mobile phone. To make an international call, dial 00, then the country code. Calls from hotels are far more expensive than calling from outside; look for the (ever increasing) call offices offering cheap rates to call overseas.

Tipping Service charge is not usually added to the check (but do make sure), and so it's customary to leave a tip of between 10–12% and more if the service has been great. If paying by credit card, it is recommended to leave a cash tip, which service staff are more likely to receive. For small cafés and snacks, a few coins or rounded up to the nearest euro is usual. For taxi drivers, a small tip is welcome but not necessary, and for hotel porters and cleaners, a small tip is always welcome but not obligatory.

Toilets It's easy to avoid the public toilets on the street (usually dismal and dirty) by running into hotels, bars, shopping centers, and department stores instead.

Tourist Information Dublin Tourism ☎ 01-605 7700. Offices: Suffolk St. (main office), Monday–Saturday 9am–5.30pm, Sunday 10.30am–3pm; June– August, Monday–Saturday 9am– 7pm, July & August Sunday 10.30am–5pm. Also on Upper O'Connell St.: 9–5pm. Both offices have bookings, maps, reservations, gift shop, all-Ireland information, and accommodation reservations service. There is an information desk at the arrivals hall in Dublin Airport.

Travelers With Disabilities

Restaurants, hotels, buses, and stations are increasingly accessible to wheelchair users, especially since hosting the Special Olympics in 2003. All new buildings take wheelchair access into account; you may find that older buildings do less so. Most taxi companies will have some vehicles that can access wheelchairs; phone to check. Phone ahead when visiting restaurants and hotels to confirm their facilities. Useful organizations include the **Irish Wheelchair Association** (www.iwa.ie).

Dublin: **A Brief History**

600 BC The Celts first arrive in Ireland.

AD 432 St Patrick arrives in Ireland and establishes the first Roman Catholic church—perhaps at the site of St Patrick's Cathedral—and converts the Irish.

837 The Vikings arrive in Dublin, using the permanent settlement as a base to plunder surrounding regions.

1014 Brian Boru, high King of Ireland, defeats the Vikings at the battle of Clontarf.

1169 The Normans capture Dublin, led by Strongbow.

1541 Henry VIII declared King of Ireland, and tries to introduce Protestantism.

1649 Oliver Cromwell's army lands in Dublin, and then kills thousands in Drogheda. Land is taken from Catholic landowners and distributed around Cromwell's Protestant supporters.

1695 Penal laws restrict education for Catholics and prohibit them from buying property.

1727 Catholics deprived the right to vote.

1759 Guinness Brewery is established in St James's Gate.

1801 The Act of Union joins England to Ireland, prohibiting Catholics from holding public office.

1829 Daniel O'Connell, a Catholic lawyer, organizes the Catholic Association, helping to achieve the Catholic Emancipation Act.

1845 The start of the Great Potato Famine: over a million people die and more emigrate on America-bound boats from Dublin's docks.

1913 Jim Larkin, head of the Trade Union movement, leads the workers in the Great Lockout.

1914 Outbreak of World War I, delaying implementation of new Home Rule legislation.

1916 Nationalists stage Easter Rising, seizing the GPO and proclaiming an independent Irish Republic. British cruch the rising and most of its leaders are executed.

1919 Beginning of the Irish War of Independence against Britain; Eamonn De Valera leads the nationalist movement Sinn Féin.

1920 British Parliament passes Government of Ireland Act, with 1 parliament for the 6 counties of Northern Ireland and 1 for the rest of Ireland.

1921 Anglo-Irish Treaty establishes the Irish Free State, partitioned from Northern Ireland.

1922 Dublin parliament ratifies the treaty, leading to civil war between the IRA and Free State army, killing hundreds. Michael Collins assassinated.

1923 Irish Free State joins the League of Nations.

1926 De Valera founds Fianna Fáil.

1927 De Valera enters parliament leading Fianna Fáil.

1932 Fianna Fáil wins General Election with De Valera head of government, and tries to eliminate British influence in Irish Free State.

1937 Fianna Fáil wins another election, and Irish Free State is abolished, proclaiming Eire (Gaelic for Ireland) as a sovereign state, with 32 counties.

1938 Douglas Hyde becomes first president of Eire; De Valera is first prime minister.

1939 Outbreak of World War II; Eire remains neutral but many Irish citizens join the Allied Forces.

1948 Fianna Fáil loses General Election; Dublin parliament passes Republic of Ireland Bill.

1949 Easter Monday, anniversary of 1916 Uprising, Eire becomes Republic of Ireland and leaves the British Commonwealth.

1955 Ireland joins the United Nations, but not NATO because of Northern Ireland's status as part of the UK.

1959 De Valera becomes president of the Republic of Ireland.

1973 Ireland joins the European Economic Community (later known as the European Union).

1980s Dublin suffers the effects of severe economic problems, with high unemployment and rising debts. Many emigrate for better opportunities.

1985 Anglo-Irish Agreement is signed, giving Republic of Ireland a role in the government of Northern Ireland.

1986 Irish budget airline Ryanair's first flight from Dublin to London, quickly spreading routes to and from Europe and increasing tourism.

1990 Mary Robinson becomes first woman president of Ireland.

1991 Ireland signs the Treaty on European Union at Maastricht.

1990s Dublin booms: Economic prosperity transforms Ireland (characterized as the Celtic Tiger) from one of Europe's poorest nations to one of its most successful. A time of immigration, rather than emigration.

1992 Ireland votes to loosen the strict abortion law, allowing travel abroad for an abortion.

1993 Downing Street Declaration: Irish and British prime ministers begin the peace process on Northern Ireland.

1997 Divorce becomes legal in Ireland, although opposed by the Roman Catholic Church.

2002 The Euro replaces the punt as Ireland's currency.

2004 Smoking is banned in all public places, including bars and restaurants. Publicans fear that this will lead to a drop in revenue.

2004 Ireland, holder of the EU presidency, welcomes 10 new member states. Dublin sees the start of a growth of Polish workers.

2007 Bertie Ahern wins third term in office as prime minister, and forms a coalition. Green Party enters government for the first time.

Dublin's **Architecture**

Medieval (12th–13th centuries AD)

Although the Vikings most certainly made their presence felt after their arrival in the 9th century, little remains of anything so early. In fact, most remains of the Viking settlement were only discovered during the "Battle of Wood Quay", when Dublin Corporation unearthed the site in the 1970s during excavation, but then insisted on building over it despite huge public pressure.

The grand **Christ Church Cathedral** existed from the Viking times, but was rebuilt by the Normans in the 12th century. The earliest sections surviving are the transept and the crypt, which extends the full length of the cathedral, and once contained three chapels. The Romanesque doorway on the south transept has intricate Irish stonework. Nearby **St Patrick's Cathedral** was built in the 13th century but, again, has been constructed so many times that little remains of its medieval past, apart from the Romanesque door. Only the section of the choir gives a hint of the old style. **St Audoen's Church** is Dublin's oldest surviving church, containing part of the original city wall. St Audoen's Arch, in its grounds, is the last surviving entrance to the old city.

Post Restoration (17th–18th centuries)

Ireland's first great classical building was **Royal Hospital Kilmainham**, inspired by Hôtel des Invalides in Paris, designed by **William Robinson** and now home to the Irish Museum of Modern Art. A huge

quadrangle built around a court-yard, it has an arcade at ground level. Similar in style is the flat-fronted **Collins Barracks**, built in the early 18th century by **Thomas Burgh**, his first recorded building, with arcaded colon-nades on 2 sides of the square.

After the Royal Hospital, this was Dublin's earliest public building. Robinson then created the façade of the small but perfectly formed **Marsh's Library**, typical of a 17th-century scholar's library with decorative oak bookcases.

Georgian (18th century)

Dublin is best known for Georgian architecture, and its enduring image is of flat-fronted brick 4- or 5-storey terraces, usually planned around a private (as then) square. A time when the affluent Protestant gentry were only too happy to improve the city, it was the symme-try and harmony of classical archi-tecture that formed the basis for this style. The **Gardner** family were the most influential of the private developers, and laid out Parnell Square, Mountjoy Square, and Hen-rietta Street, which meant the north side was, for a short time, the city's most fashionable area. The city's town houses were brick-built with a basement and symmetrically arranged windows that got shorter the higher up to give the illusion of greater height. The best examples today can be seen at **Merrion Square**, which these days is very much a *des res*. The fanlights over

the front door, and how ornate they were, indi-cated the wealth and pres-tige of the owner. They may have looked unadorned from the outside, but plasterers extraordinaire enhanced every-thing, such as **La Franchini** brothers (Newman House).

In addition to the residential squares and terraces, the era was also marked by **James Gandon's Custom House** and the **Four Courts**, both on the Liffey's north bank. Both of these grand buildings were built in the classi-cal style with domes, ornate decora-tion, and symbolic sculpture adorning the gateways.

Notable architects of the time were German-born **Richard Cassels**, who worked on the **Houses of Parliament** and **Leinster House** built for the Earl of Kildare. **Sir**

Edward Lovett Pearce is the main man behind Palladianism in Ireland, including the **Houses of Parliament** (now the bank of Ireland).

Victorian (19th century)

There are relatively few Victorian masterpieces around the city, as Dublin suffered a decline following the Act of Union, but those that remain make their mark. The stunning red-brick **George's Street Arcade** was Dublin's first and only Victorian shopping center, with ornate Gothic exterior. Traditional bars are the best way of seeing Victorian architecture and interior design, those with rarely-changed Victorian interiors including **Ryan's** and the **Stag's Head**, all mahogany paneling and snugs, to keep the drinking discrete.

Modern (20th century to present)

The most famous (infamous) new

addition to Dublin's architectural scene is **The Spire**, causing mayhem when it was completed in 2002 to mark the new Millennium (late). The stainless steel spire is 120m (366 ft) high and the tallest structure in Dublin. Other slightly less controversial modern-day buildings include the **IFSC**, the International Financial Services Centre, the modern-day powerhouse of Ireland's vibrant economy, and the first phase of the Dublin Corporation Offices by Sam Stephenson, one of Dublin's best known contemporary architects. New creations around the docklands include **Grand Canal Square** designed by **Martha Schwartz**.

Toll-free Numbers and Websites

Airlines

AER LINGUS
☎ 800-474 7424 in the US & Canada
☎ 0818-365 000 in Ireland
☎ 0870-876 5000 in the UK
www.aerlingus.com

AER ARANN
☎ 0818-210 210 in Ireland
☎ 0870-876 7676 in the UK
www.aerarann.com

AIR FRANCE
☎ 800-237 2747 in the US
☎ 01-605 0383 in Ireland
www.airfrance.com

*AIR SOUTHWEST
☎ 0870-241 8202 in the UK
www.airsouthwest.com

ALITALIA
☎ 800-223 5730 in the US
www.alitalia.it

AMERICAN AIRLINES
☎ 800-433 7300 in the US
☎ 01-602 0550 in Ireland
www.aa.com

*BMI
☎ 800-788 0555 in the US
☎ 0870-607 0555 in the UK
www.flybmi.com

BRITISH AIRWAYS
☎ 800-247 9297 in the US
☎ 1890-626 747 in Ireland
☎ 0870-850 9850 in the UK
www.ba.com

CONTINENTAL AIRLINES
☎ 800-231 0856 in the US
☎ 1890-925 252 in Ireland
www.continental.com

DELTA AIRLINES
☎ 800-241 4141 in the US
☎ 01-407 3165 in Ireland
www.delta.com

*FLYBE
☎ 0871-522 6100 in the UK
www.flybe.com

KLM
☎ 020-4 747 747 in the Netherlands
www.klm.com

LUFTHANSA
☎ 800-399 5838 in the US
☎ 01-844 5544 from Ireland

NORTHWEST AIRLINES
☎ 800-225 2525 in the US
www.nwa.com

QANTAS
☎ 800-227 4500 in the US
☎ 01-407 3278 in Ireland
www.qantas.com

*RYANAIR
☎ 0818-303030 in Ireland
☎ 0871-246 0000 in the UK
www.ryanair.com

UNITED AIRLINES
☎ 800-538 2929 in the US
www.united.com

SAS
☎ 800-221 2350 in the US
☎ 844-5440 in Ireland
www.flysas.com

US AIRWAYS
☎ 800-622 1015 in the US
☎ 1890-925 065 in Ireland
www.usairways.com

VIRGIN ATLANTIC
☎ 800-821 5438 in the US
☎ 08705-747 747 in the UK
www.virgin-atlantic.com

* indicates an Internet-based airline.

Car-hire agencies

ALAMO
☎ 800-327 9633
☎ 01-844 4162 in Ireland
www.goalamo.com

AVIS
☎ 800-331 1212 in the US
☎ 01-605 7500 in Dublin
www.avis.com

BUDGET

☎ 800-527 0700 in the US
☎ 9066-27711 in Ireland
www.budget.com

NATIONAL

☎ 800-227 3876 in the US
☎ 01-844 4162 in Ireland
www.nationalcar.co.uk

THRIFTY

☎ 800-367 2277 in the US
☎ 01-844 1944 in Ireland
www.thrifty.com

Index

See also Accommodations and Restaurant indexes, below.

Photo **Credits**